D0153880

COMEDY

What is comedy? Andrew Stott traces changing definitions of the term from Aristotle to Chris Morris's *Brass Eye* via Oscar Wilde and *Some Like It Hot*. Providing readers with the ideal critical introduction to the irrepressible genre of comedy, this wide-ranging and thorough overview:

- investigates comic forms, theories, and techniques
- considers comic identity, including that of clowns, stereotypes, and the stand-up comic
- introduces comedy's role in theories of deconstruction, psychoanalysis, and gender
- features analytical case studies on a number of themes, from political satire to slapstick
- considers comic representations of the body and sexuality
- reviews theories of the cultural and psychological purposes of laughter

Introducing complex theoretical ideas in an accessible and lively way, this is the essential guide for those studying comedy in its many forms.

Andrew Stott is Assistant Professor of English at the State University of New York, Buffalo.

THE NEW CRITICAL IDIOM

SERIES EDITOR: JOHN DRAKAKIS, UNIVERSITY OF STIRLING

The New Critical Idiom is an invaluable series of introductory guides to today's critical terminology. Each book

- provides a handy, explanatory guide to the use (and abuse) of the term
- offers an original and distinctive overview by a leading literary and cultural critic
- relates the term to the larger field of cultural representation.

With a strong emphasis on clarity, lively debate, and the widest possible breadth of examples, *The New Critical Idiom* is an indispensable approach to key topics in literary studies.

Also available in this series:

COMEDY

Andrew Stott

Routledge
Taylor & Francis Group

NEW YORK AND LONDON

First published 2005
by Routledge
270 Madison Ave, New York, NY 10016

Simultaneously published in the UK
by Routledge
2 Park Square, Milton Park, Abingdon, Oxon OX14 4RN

Routledge is an imprint of the Taylor & Francis Group

© 2005 Andrew Stott

Typeset in Adobe Garamond and Scala Sans by Keystroke,
Jacaranda Lodge, Wolverhampton
Printed and bound in Great Britain by
TJ International Ltd, Padstow, Cornwall

Library of Congress Cataloging in Publication Data
Stott, Andrew, 1969–
   Comedy / Andrew Stott.
      p.   cm. – (The new critical idiom)
   Includes bibliographical references and index.
   1. Comedy. I. Title. II. Series.
   PN1922.S78 2005
   809'.917–dc22   2004010093

British Library Cataloguing in Publication Data
A catalogue record for this book is available from the British Library

ISBN 0–415–29932–2 (hbk)
ISBN 0–415–29933–0 (pbk)

CONTENTS

SERIES EDITOR'S PREFACE

The New Critical Idiom is a series of introductory books which seeks to extend the lexicon of literary terms, in order to address the radical changes which have taken place in the study of literature during the last decades of the twentieth century. The aim is to provide clear, well-illustrated accounts of the full range of terminology currently in use, and to evolve histories of its changing usage.

The current state of the discipline of literary studies is one where there is considerable debate concerning basic questions of terminology. This involves, among other things, the boundaries which distinguish the literary from the non-literary; the position of literature within the larger sphere of culture; the relationship between literatures of different cultures; and questions concerning the relation of literary to other cultural forms within the context of interdisciplinary studies.

It is clear that the field of literary criticism and theory is a dynamic and heterogeneous one. The present need is for individual volumes on terms which combine clarity of exposition with an adventurousness of perspective and a breadth of application. Each volume will contain as part of its apparatus some indication of the direction in which the definition of particular terms is likely to move, as well as expanding the disciplinary boundaries within which some of these terms have been traditionally contained. This will involve some re-situation of terms within the larger field of cultural representation, and will introduce examples from the area of film and the modern media in addition to examples from a variety of literary texts.

ACKNOWLEDGEMENTS

In keeping with the communal spirit of comedy, this book is the product of a number of good-natured interactions and has benefited greatly from the assistance of the following people: Keith Hindle and Nigel Mapp were kind enough to comment extensively on drafts, and without the profit of their rigorous and generous readings, this work would be much impaired. Monica Kendall also furnished excellent comments on my final draft. Terry Hawkes graciously allowed me to borrow a bit on Simon Forman I heard him deliver at a meeting of the London Shakespeare Seminar in 2002. Liz Thompson at Routledge is to be thanked for giving me the opportunity to write the book in the first place, and for retaining always the virtue of patient and good-humoured correspondence while I moved countries and generally didn't get down to it. John Drakakis has offered consistently supportive and authoritative editorial advice from first to last, and I am delighted to appear in his series. The final and most outstanding debt of gratitude is owed to Josie Stott, the funniest person I know, whose love, encouragement and support make everything worth doing. For this, and everything else, I love you.

INTRODUCTION

> Tragedy is when I cut my finger. Comedy is when you fall down an
> open sewer and die.
>
> Mel Brooks

Providing a simple formula to answer the question 'what is comedy?' is
not so easy. On the one hand, comedy is a reasonably graspable literary
form, most properly applied to drama, that uses stock character types
in a scenario where some kind of problem must be resolved. Comedies
end happily, often concluding with a communal celebration such as
a feast or a marriage. We might add that we would expect a comedy to be
funny, and that during the course of its action no one will be killed.
But this definition is fine just so long as we understand comedy in its
strictest and most restrictive sense within literary history. In his study
of five centuries of English stage comedy, Alexander Leggatt notes the
relative stability of this formula across generations of writers, describing
it as our most consistent literary genre, 'surviving centuries of cultural
change with its basic conventions stubbornly intact' (Leggatt, 1998: 1).
Yet any consideration of what we think of as comedy in the modern
day exposes numerous anomalies and deviations from this pattern, and
a diversity of linguistic and performance practices. As a label, 'comedy'
can be applied across a range of styles, including traditional categories such

as pastoral comedy, farce, burlesque, pantomime, satire, and the comedy of manners; yet it also applies to more modern subdivisions: cartoons, sitcom, sketch comedy, slapstick cinema, stand-up, some game shows, impressionists, caricatures, and even silly walks. Applying a single uniform definition or methodological approach to such a mixture would be highly unsatisfactory. This terminological range is a product of the fact that comedy is as much a tonal quality as a structural one. While there is a long-standing literary tradition of comedy, 'the comic' is an identifiable mode or tone of writing that manifests itself in a multitude of media, genres, and forms that are not necessarily synonymous with comedy. The mixture of comic with tragic and other elements in writers as diverse as Shakespeare, Dickens, Ibsen, Samuel Beckett, Carol Churchill, or Martin Amis, for example, is indicative of what W. Moelwyn Merchant called the 'permanently recurring affront to the purity of comedy and tragedy as dramatic categories' (Merchant, 1972: 1). In postmodernism, parody, burlesque, and satire – notably 'comic' techniques – are used in the service of serious critiques of Enlightenment philosophy. In practice, then, generic definitions show themselves to be porous, and we often see comic business appearing in contexts structurally inconsistent with that form. This might lead us to suggest that what we call comedy is really humour, a specific tone operating free from generic restraints, which, while not the exclusive property of comedy is closely associated with it. Similarly, laughter, the most immediate meter of comedy's success or failure, does not belong to it uniquely, and is equally induced by humour but also embarrassment, fear, guilt, tickling, or laughing gas.

By retaining a broader understanding of the term comedy we can use it as a means of organizing and understanding a series of persistent themes that we encounter again and again across a variety of settings. These themes include various forms of inversion, the 'world-turned-upside-down' scenario where slave governs master or man bites dog. Foolishness, intellectual myopia, or the rigid insistence on inflexible systems of being or thinking are ridiculed by transformations of different kinds, investigations of alternative identities, or a relaxation of social codes and a suspension of laws governing the body. The matter-of-fact comprehensibility of language is compromised by linguistic contortions that produce parallel or nonsensical forms of meaning. In all these, regardless of where they appear, a notion of 'comedy' is at work. That our understanding of it is not contained by one definition or narrative arc is one of the principles of this book. 'Comedy' is a term that can refer equally to a genre, a tone, and a series of effects that manifest themselves in diverse environments. This will require us to think of comedy multilaterally, as at once a literary tradition with identifiable structural qualities, and as a way of describing isolated events or passages within other types of work.

As a dramatic form, the historical development of comedy appears to confirm the idea of a relatively permeable form adapting to suit the demands of the day. Cordatus, the moderator of Ben Jonson's play *Every Man Out of His Humour* (1600), offers us this synopsis of its development from its origins in ancient ritual:

> 'tis extant, that that which we call *Comoedia*, was at first nothing but a simple and continued Satyre, sung by one only person, till *Susario* invented a second, after him, *Epicharmus* a third; *Phormus* and *Chionides* devised to have foure actors, with a *Prologue* and *Chorus*; to which *Cratinus* (long after), added a fifth and sixt; *Eupolis*, more, *Aristophanes*, more than they: every man in the dignity of his spirit and judgment, supplied something: and (though that in him this kind of Poeme appeared absolute, and fully perfected) yet how is the face of it chang'd since, in *Menander*, *Philemon*, *Cecilius*, *Plautus*, and the rest; who have utterly excluded the *Chorus*, altered the property of the persons, their names, and natures, and augmented it with all libertie, according to the elegancie and disposition of those times wherein they wrote?
>
> (Jonson, 1920: Induction, 261–275)

In this version, comedy begins as a simple song for a lone voice gradually accumulating protagonists and interlocutors as each authorial generation presents additions to the form. In this, Jonson, whose own comedies were innovative and markedly different from those that preceded him, suggests that comedy is by definition open to continual adaptation. It offers a welcome opportunity for greater freedom of expression:

> I see not then, but we should enjoy the same *Licentia*, or free power to illustrate and heighten our invention, as they did; and not be tied to

those strict and regular forms which the niceness of a fewe (who are nothing but Forme), would thrust upon us.

(Jonson, 1920: Induction, 275–279)

Our knowledge of the origins and development of comedy has not advanced far beyond Jonson's. A clue to its beginnings may be found in the etymology of the word itself, which is generally agreed to be derived from an amalgamation of the Greek words '*kômos*' or '*kômaî*', and '*odà*', words that reflect comedy's roots in the Greek peninsula. '*Kômos*' translates as 'revel', while '*kômaî*' comes from the word for 'village'. Aristotle (*c*.384–322 BC) preferred this second definition, remarking that the Dorians 'call outlying villages *kômai* . . . the assumption being that comedians were so-called not from the revel or *kômos*, but because they toured the villages when expelled from the town in disgrace' (Aristotle, 1996: 6). '*Odà*' is uncontroversially translated as 'song', and so comedy is either a hymn of celebration or, as Dante (1265–1321) styled it, 'a rustic song' (Dante, 1984: 31). Most critics and historians agree that comedy appears to be the product of a rural environment rather than an urban one, and to have come into being in association with seasonal agrarian fertility rites. At some stage, comedy also began a long association with the god Dionysus, whose divine characteristics and patronage are clearly impressed on the form. Dionysus, the son of Zeus and Semele, was originally a god of the fertility of nature, a vegetation-spirit who died and was reborn yearly. His cult reached Greece from either Thrace or Phrygia at around 1000 BC, and was particularly notable for its devotional use of wine and the orgiastic revels of its votaries, especially women, who withdrew into the wild to make contact with nature. Dionysus was often described as having a minor god, Phales, as his companion, of whom little is known except his obvious association with the word 'phallus', and by the fourth century BC Dionysus had outgrown his association with organic fertility to become a sponsor of human sexual behaviour. The temperament and qualities of Dionysus and the nature of his worship appear, then, to have exerted a significant degree of influence on the principles of festivity, inversion, relative sexual freedom, and travesty that we find in comedy. Also significant is the removal from the city he encourages, placing him at the fringes of the civic environment and drawing his followers away from urban jurisdiction and inducing them into conduct that would be unacceptable in the city. Echoes of these Dionysial themes can still be heard much later on, as in the libidity, rusticity, and altered consciousness of *A Midsummer Night's Dream* (1595). Dionysus' most important function in terms of the literary history of comedy was as the patron of both the Lenaea and the 'Great Dionysia', annual Athenian theatrical festivals at which prizes were awarded to the best dramatists. Initially, the Dionysia, the more important of the two, were only for tragedians, with comedies performed only at the winter Lenaea. From around 486 BC, a comedy competition was initiated at the Dionysia, the point at which we may say that comedy is institutionalized as a significant literary form. We can say this because the Dionysia appear to have played an important role as a civic gathering and statement of national identity aside the presentation of theatrics, a platform where the achievements of the state might be annually reiterated, honours granted to citizens of distinction, and the lines of social division and hierarchy be graphically represented in terms of seating and participation. A sense of collective involvement in the issues of government might also be raised through the debates aired in plays (Palmer, 1994: 31–32).

This leads us to a further question asked of comedy: what purpose does it serve, and what, if anything, is its social function or philosophical value, apart from giving pleasure? While the comedy of Aristophanes (*c.*448–380 BC) sustained an overt political and satirical commentary, comic drama was encouraged to move away from current affairs at an early stage in its development. Aristotle tells us that it was Crates (active 450 BC) who 'first abandoned the form of a lampoon and began to construct universalized stories and plots'; and by the time of Menander (*c.*342–*c.*291 BC) nearly a century later, comedy had ceased to intervene in the issues of government, at least explicitly (Aristotle, 1996: 9). Instead, comedy was commended for its realistic representation of the human condition, famously moving the early Alexandrine scholar Aristophanes of Byzantium to ask, 'O Menander and Life / Which of you is imitating which?' (Segal, 2001: 153). By the fourth century AD, the idea of comedy as an instructive literary form takes shape in the work of Donatus, a grammarian who taught at Rome, and who wrote enormously influential remarks on the comedies of Terence, works he would have never seen performed and would have only known as texts. Under these sterile conditions, Donatus declared comedy to be essentially didactic, mirroring everyday life and schooling us in practical ethics. He also emphasized the academic qualities of comedy, arguing that good comedy should be built according to sound rhetorical principles (Herrick, 1950: 65). Donatus' scholarly and moralistic method fortified comedy with some of the technical respectability of tragedy, and the principal arguments of comic theory from the Renaissance onwards are based on his ideas. That its primary function is corrective is argued in 1698, for example, by William Congreve in response to the clergyman Jeremy Collier's attack on him in particular and theatre in general. 'Men are to be laughed out of their vices in comedy', he wrote. 'The business of comedy is to delight as well as to instruct; and as vicious people are made ashamed of their follies and faults by seeing them exposed in a ridiculous manner, so are good people at once both warned and diverted at their expense' (Congreve, 1997a: 515). Two centuries later, in his 'Essay on Comedy' (1877), the playwright George Meredith made a similar point, although metaphysically enlarging it by personifying comedy as a benign spirit monitoring human behaviour. 'Whenever they wax out of proportion, overblown, affected, pretentious, bombastical, hypocritical, pedantic, fantastically delicate', he writes,

> whenever it sees them self-deceived or hoodwinked, given to run riot in idolatries, drifting into vanities, congregating in absurdities, planning short-sightedly, plotting dementedly; whenever they are at variance with their professions, and violate the unwritten but perceptible laws binding them in consideration one to another; whenever they offend sound reason, fair justice; are false in humility or mined with conceit . . . the Spirit overhead will look humanely malign, and cast an oblique light on them, followed by volleys of silvery laughter. That is the Comic Spirit.
>
> (Meredith, 1980: 48)

The extent to which we have been profitably instructed, or productively chastised by this 'humanely malign' creature is deeply debatable, especially in the present day.

In the twentieth century, critics have been less keen to subscribe to comedy's didacticism. Some, like Maurice Charney, see a central method-ological absence in contemporary discussions of the form that leaves us with 'no common assumptions and no set of conventions by which we could agree on how to speak about comedy' (Charney, 1978: vii–viii).

More assertive critics, like Harry Levin, see comedy as a conflict between the emotions of joviality and sobriety, a 'perennial war of the laughers against the non-laughers', of playboys against killjoys, 'locked in an eternal battle of world views' (Levin, 1987: 40). For Erich Segal, the history of Western comedy plots a long line of descent from the euphoric highs of 'Aristophanic triumph' to the resignation of the 'theatre of inadequacy', represented by the work of Samuel Beckett. According to this thesis, vigorous expressions of life begin to fade and become more complicated and contingent as history and experience instruct us in cynicism, and boisterous, optimistic comic forms are rendered increasingly untenable. Beckett's *Waiting for Godot* (1953) epitomizes comedy's fate:

> The drama will have no happy ending. Indeed, it will have no ending at all. There will be no revel, renewal, or rejuvenation. For whatever Godot may represent, whether salvation or erotic rebirth, one thing is clear. The traditional happy ending is no longer possible – because comedy is dead.
>
> (Segal, 2001: 452)

Rather than proposing narratives of comic function that are intended to hold true in all times and places, some critics, especially those with an interest in poststructuralist theory, are drawn to its apparent indefiniteness and resistance to definition. Andrew Horton claims that 'like language, and like "texts" in general, the comic is plural, unfinalized, disseminative, dependent on *context* and the intertextuality of creator, text, and contemplator' (Horton, 1991: 9). Kirby Olson adopts a similar approach, reading comic fiction through the work of twentieth-century French philosophers Jean-François Lyotard and Gilles Deleuze, and finding in comedy an affront to rationality and meta-narratives that attempt to exhaustively explain or incorporate all aspects of the world:

> Comedy is an immanent form that does not make us look into the heavens or to God for answers to questions. . . . Comic theory traces a larger discourse over politics of the body and, within that discourse, between orthodoxy and heresy. Like desire, laughter is strangely fluid and cannot be contained by rational thought.
>
> (Olson, 2001: 5)

For Olson, the slippery problem of defining comedy and comic action satisfactorily is evidence of its postmodern virtues: 'Comedy is precisely *a certain freedom from definition*' (Olson, 2001: 6, original emphasis).

Perhaps the only formulation that remains appropriate is also one of the vaguest. In 1900, the French metaphysician Henri Bergson, of whom much more in Chapter 6, argued that 'the comic does not exist outside the pale of what is strictly *human*', a statement that maintains that in all instances, events must at some point intersect with human consciousness to become comic (Bergson, 1980: 62). The humanness of comedy was noted by Aristotle who observed that we are the only creatures who feel compelled to laugh. Comedy is certainly a social activity first and foremost, conceived of always with some kind of audience in mind, and everywhere produced from the matter of dominant cultural assumptions and commonplaces. The question of *how* or *why* things come to be funny is similarly determined by culture. Even though comedy often seems to be suspending, inverting, or abandoning dominant norms, these inversions are produced in relation to the cultural orthodoxies from which they must always begin. It should therefore be possible to trace comic events back to the significations they have transformed. In this way, the comic can be thought of as a means of opening up the possibility of multiple perspectives, as each concept culturally established as orthodox simultaneously presents itself for the possibility of comic subversion, like a silent but parallel conversation that could audibly erupt at any moment. Take the traditional story of the Greek poet Philomon, who, we are told, died laughing after he saw a donkey eating figs. The lethal quality of this scene was the perceived incongruity of a beast eating what was categorized as human food. What killed Philomon, therefore, was an event that violated certain prefabricated categories of decorum and appropriateness applicable to figs and donkeys, coupled with his ability to perceive that violation as ludicrous and culminating in dangerously high levels of amusement. We can understand this as an experience of division within the poet that allowed him to interpret multiple layers of significance instantaneously and simultaneously. For Bergson, the division between the perceived and the actual, and the possibility of reading situations in a number of different ways, was a phenomenon he isolated as one of the three principal triggers of laughter. What he labelled 'the reciprocal interference of series' is a scenario that 'belongs simultaneously to two altogether independent series of events and is capable of being interpreted in two entirely different meanings at the same time' (Bergson, 1980: 122). Examples would include Oliver Goldsmith's play *She Stoops to Conquer* (1773), where Marlow mistakes the Hardcastle's house for an inn, or the film *Monty Python's Life of Brian* (1979), where Brian's life parallels that of Jesus Christ, and he is mistaken for the son of God. What is amusing is the tension caused by the coexistence and interplay between 'the double fact of coincidence and interference' (Bergson, 1980: 124), such as Brian's unwittingly amassing a devout following while his mother insists that 'he's not the messiah, he's a very naughty boy'. That both Brian's followers and his mother should be confirmed in their contrasting beliefs is made plausible by the setting and the action of the film, and thus *Life of Brian* demonstrates a continual awareness of the possibility of reading a scenario in two different ways, of a division in comprehension and the coexistence of parallel ideas.

The theme of comedy as a divided and doubled experience is even embodied for us in the double act, a staple of comic performance since the appearance of Dionysus and his servant Xanthias in Aristophanes' *Frogs* (405 BC). Double acts present a perfect embodiment of the uneasy doubling and bifocal perceptions of comedy. Similarly, we might look to the disparity between place and self that is continually used in comedy, stories in which people are geographically, linguistically, or, in some profound existential way, misplaced, 'fish out of water' comedies like Molière's *Le Bourgeois Gentilhomme* (1670), Buster Keaton's *The General* (1926), Eddie Murphy's *Trading Places* (1983), or Steve Martin's *Bringing Down the House* (2003). Another stock situation presents a discrepancy between the way a character presents him- or herself and the substance of their actions, as is the case with Shakespeare's pompous Falstaff, or the hypocritical devout in Molière's *Tartuffe* (1664). A recurring technique of the comedy team Monty Python (1969–74) was the discussion of quotidian topics in an elevated register, exploiting discontinuity between form and content, as in this sports report that blends philosophy with soccer:

> Last night in . . . Jarrow, we witnessed the resuscitation of a great footballing tradition, when Jarrow United came of age, in a European sense, with an almost Proustian display of modern existentialist football.

> Virtually annihilating by midfield moral argument the now surely obso-
> lescent catennachio defensive philosophy of Signor Alberto Fanfrino.
> Bologna indeed were a side intellectually out argued by a Jarrow team
> thrusting and bursting with aggressive Kantian positivism.
>
> (Chapman *et al.*, 1998, vol. 1: 139)

All these examples utilize some form of incongruity, and rely upon a
culturally defined sense of incompatible orders, such as the displacement
of people or discourses, to produce ambiguity and the feeling that
normality has been momentarily decentred for pleasurable ends. This has
been studied by Mary Douglas in her work on joking relationships in
traditional cultures. Douglas argues that a joke cannot simply jump from
nowhere, but derives from a sense of reality that pre-exists it, and which
it seeks to distort:

> a joke is seen and allowed when it offers a symbolic pattern of a social
> pattern occurring at the same time . . . all jokes are expressive of the
> social situations in which they occur. The one social condition necessary
> for a joke to be enjoyed is that the social group in which it is received
> should develop the formal characteristics of a 'told' joke: that is a
> dominant pattern of relation is challenged by another. If there is no joke
> in the social structure, no other joking can appear.
>
> (Douglas, 1975: 98)

Jokes therefore emerge from within the social framework and necessarily express the nature of their environment, which means that all
jokes are necessarily produced in a relative relationship to the dominant
structures of understanding and the epistemological order. Despite the
violation of the social order implied by joking, the joker enjoys a kind of
immunity through the belief that his or her wit represents insight into a
different type of consciousness:

> The joker's own immunity can be derived philosophically from his
> apparent access to other reality than that mediated by the relevant
> structure. Such access is implied in the contrast of forms in which he
> deals. His jokes expose the inadequacy of realist structurings of
> experience and so release the pent-up power of the imagination.
>
> (Douglas, 1975: 108)

Douglas's conclusions suggest that joking is an imaginative exploration of alternative social formulations, and a recognition of lack in the 'realist structurings of experience' that usually represent it. Through joking, the joker appears to gain privileged insight beyond the social construct where its meanings are neither exhaustive nor absolute, but are simply choices. Joking reveals the practical limits of cultural structures; for all systemic choices, other choices could have been made.

Joking is quite different in Freudian psychoanalysis, but nevertheless similarly revealing of an underside to socially constructed 'reason'. For Sigmund Freud, a joke is an example of 'parapraxis', an act like a mistake or slip of the tongue that exposes something of the repressed thoughts hidden in the unconscious. Like dreams, jokes contain significant information about unconscious thoughts and the nature of inhibitions, and the production of a joke is a means of negotiating the psychological barrier between the conscious and unconscious mind. Freud points out that jokes have a tendency to spring from nowhere, suddenly appearing like little emissaries of the unconscious. 'A joke', he writes,

> has quite outstandingly the characteriztic of being a notion that has occurred to us 'involuntarily'. What happens is not that we know a moment beforehand what joke we are going to make, and that all it then needs is to be clothed in words. We have an indefinable feeling, rather, which I can best compare with an '*absence*', a sudden release of intellectual tension, and then all at once the joke is there – as a rule ready clothed in words.
>
> (Freud [1905], 2001: 167, original emphasis)

Making jokes is an almost involuntary act; they come across the joker in an instant, fully formed and with no explanation as to how they were made. In Freud's analysis, joking is symptomatic of the division in the psyche that characterizes human beings. Once again, the comic acts as a parallel conversation, tracking reason and occasionally interrupting it.

So what does this strange ability simultaneously to recognize the social order and comically subvert it amount to? Existential philosopher Helmuth Plessner cites the perception of the comic as evidence that human beings are intrinsically '*eccentric*', as they are the only animals with the capacity to reflect on their thoughts and experiences. Plessner argues that our experience of the world is a result of information mediated through the purposeful management of our speech, thoughts, and control of our limbs, all of which, organized around a coherent sense of self, leads us to believe in our mastery of the immediate environment. The world outside, however, is unconcerned with the individual ego, and treats the human body as yet more matter. Thus we are at once convinced of our control of the environment, but simultaneously aware that we are subject to disinterested nature:

> Just as the world and my own body are revealed to me, and can be controlled by me, only insofar as they appear in relation to me as a central 'I', so, on the other hand, they retain their ascendancy over their subjection in this perspective as an order indifferent to me and including me in a nexus of mutual neighbourhoods.
>
> (Plessner, 1970: 36)

The subject, then, comes to reflect upon itself as both ego and matter, and is divided in this knowledge. As Simon Critchley puts it, 'the human being has a reflective attitude towards its experiences and towards itself', living 'beyond the limits set for them by nature by taking up a distance from their immediate experience' (Critchley, 2002: 28). The title of Plessner's work is *Laughing and Crying*, because these effects, both largely involuntary, involve moments when the bodily intrudes into the sense of self and overruns it, disturbing the conscious mind. Human eccentricity is the product, therefore, of discontinuity between the world in our head and the world outside. 'In this respect,' says Plessner, 'man is inferior to the animal since the animal does not experience itself as shut off from its physical existence, as an inner self or I, and in consequence does not have to overcome a break between itself and itself, itself and its physical existence' (Plessner, 1970: 37). We could attribute to this phenomenon of being 'shut off' the often remarked-upon cruelty of comedy, which involves a certain degree of desensitization. If it is generically appropriate for tragedy to ask us to be sensible of human suffering, then comedy, as my Mel Brooks epigraph shows, allows us to stand back and look upon human misfortune from an emotional distance, sometimes even deriving great pleasure from it.

In a discussion of Charles Baudelaire's (1821–67) concept of irony in a 1969 essay entitled 'The Rhetoric of Temporality', literary theorist Paul de Man develops a further idea of the discontinuity between what we might understand as material nature and human consciousness. In this essay, de Man explains that Baudelaire's notion of irony is not an intersubjective concept, something produced between people, but an internalized relationship, a 'relationship, within consciousness, between two selves' (de Man, 1983: 212). Where comic relationships often imply positions of superiority and inferiority, there are no proper 'selves' within the internalized ironic relationship to occupy those spaces, and so it is not possible to think of one as 'superior' or more knowledgeable than another. Therefore, says de Man, irony 'merely designates the *distance* constitutive of all acts of reflection. Superiority and inferiority . . . become merely spatial metaphors to indicate a discontinuity and a plurality of levels within a subject that comes to know itself by an increasing differentiation from what it is not' (de Man, 1983: 213). This is especially pronounced when a human being differentiates him- or herself from the non-human world. When a person falls over, for example, the inauthentic nature of the relationship of identity to its surroundings is exposed:

> The Fall, in the literal as well as the theological sense, reminds him of the purely instrumental, reified character of his relationship to nature. Nature can at all times treat him as if he were a thing and remind him of his factitiousness, whereas he is quite powerless to convert even the smallest particle of nature into something human.
>
> (de Man, 1983: 214)

Human beings, prone to treat the world around them as if it were a thing that they could control (de Man uses the word 'reified', to suggest that nature is incorrectly perceived as a malleable commodity), find themselves made into a thing by nature. De Man continues by adding that humans largely know the world as a 'language-determined' experience, in which everything is perceived through a linguistic framework. Ironic language, the language of the Fall, is language that expresses the 'inauthentic' nature of the subject's relationship to the world:

> The ironic language splits the subject into an empirical self that exists in a state of inauthenticity and a self that exists only in the form of a language that asserts the knowledge of this inauthenticity. This does not, however, make it into an authentic language, for to know authenticity is not the same as to be authentic.
>
> (de Man, 1983: 214)

Thus in irony, the subject is divided into an inauthentic self, and a self that knows itself to be inauthentic. In various ways, all the ideas discussed above suggest that in some experience of the comic there is a division of consciousness that enables the subject to see the world with bifurcated vision. Instances of joking, humour, or irony invoke a separation between 'authorized', egocentric, or rational versions of the world and their revealed alternatives, commenting on established conventions as they go. This does not mean that joking opens up a path to 'truth', or even that it has the ability to cut through untruths, as it generally does not provide coherent counter-arguments and its efficacy as a platform for change is questionable. Indeed, we would have to say that the duality enabled in joking and comic scenarios opposes any univocal interpretation of the world. Given this principle, this book will not attempt to explain comedy in accordance with a single methodological framework or narrative of literary development. Instead, we shall approach comedy thematically, accepting what appears to be its bifurcated nature by treating it as a multifaceted and diverse series of events, rather than a generic totality, and evoking particular theories or concepts only whenever they might usefully help us to understand comic ideas.

Chapter 1 considers the reputation of comedy in academic and scholarly circles, assessing the status of the genre in works of literary criticism and the professionalized literary studies undertaken in university departments. Here we will see that the reputation of comedy suffers from both the lack of a foundational manifesto and an association with popular culture that results in its denigration and relegation in the hierarchy of literary forms. In the latter part of the twentieth century, however, certain schools of thought have developed that have re-examined the comic in the light of its socio-cultural context and declared it a fertile site of resistance and liberation.

Having sought to establish the genealogy of comedy as an object of intellectual scrutiny, the remainder of this study deals with broad themes that appear and reappear across a variety of comic texts and performances. Chapter 2 discusses the question of identity in comedy and seeks to delineate a number of popular modes of characterization, locating their origins and attempting to unpack the range of their cultural and philosophical significances. Characters such as the Native American trickster, or the medieval European figure of Folly, are shown to express contradictions in the societies from which they spring, their maddening, nonsensical, or outrageous behaviour the result of competing cultural demands intersecting in this one figure.

Extending the discussion of the previous chapter, but also limiting its focus to a specific issue, Chapter 3 deals with the treatment of gender and sexuality in comedy. This chapter is primarily interested in the representation of both orthodox and transgressive representations of sex, gender, and the interaction of men and women. As sex is probably the single most persistent theme in comedy – and we can also see that comedy has traditionally allowed the most explicit and frequent discussions of sex in the public arena – we shall consider how comic narratives consistently engage in a debate about the concept of gender and the nature of desire. Drag and transvestism are recurring themes here, and we will consider how comedies such as Shakespeare's *As You Like It*, and Billy Wilder's 1959 film *Some Like It Hot*, make much of the potential for same-sex desire that cross-dressing occasions. By way of contrast, it is also necessary that we consider the surly companionship and perpetual battle of the sexes that is marriage as represented by a range of postwar British situation comedies.

Sexuality leads us inevitably to a consideration of the body, and Chapter 4 deals with the chaotic, disruptive, and ungainly body of comedy, considering the extent to which comedy narrates a nightmare fantasy of the body in revolt. In this chapter there is also a discussion of the female body in comedy, the source of so much prurient humour, sexist remark, and cultural anxiety, attempting to outline the extent to which the female body is considered always, in a sense, inappropriate, and imagined as a site of potential moral and social subversion. Comedy has often worked according to the conventions of a literary tradition that tries to tame and moderate the female body, but in performers, such as Jennifer Saunders and Jo Brand, is now a platform from which to launch attacks on such types of repressive and conservative thinking.

Is comedy therefore a political genre? The answer is yes, and Chapter 5 discusses the extent to which comedy has been involved in political debate since its first structured manifestations in the work of Aristophanes. Politics, of course, can have many agendas and this chapter discusses satire, the way in which comedy has been used to serve reactionary ends, such as reinforcing negative racial or sexist stereotypes, and also efforts to produce a political comedy in service of the politics of the left wing. The final question of this chapter is whether or not comedy can ever be a suitable forum for the discussion of extremely sensitive and emotionally charged political issues. Considering three film comedies that look in part at the horror of the concentration camps, this chapter will evaluate the response of comic form to difficult content, and question the suitability and desirability of placing such issues alongside some degree of comic content.

The final chapter shifts the thematic focus of the book a little and considers laughter, something that does not belong to comedy exclusively but which is coupled to it to the degree that comedies without laughter are nowadays considered failed comedies. Laughter remains an inexplicable aspect of human behaviour, but there have been many attempts to either incorporate it into a theory of human nature or equate it with kinds of moral impropriety. To conclude, this chapter looks at the trope of laughter as it has been invoked in contemporary poststructuralist theory as a means of conceptualizing the limit and very edge of everything that can be said and understood.

1

COMEDY IN THE ACADEMY

> And this book – considering comedy a wondrous medicine,
> with its satire and mime, which would produce the purification of
> the passions through the enactment of defect, fault, weakness
> – would induce false scholars to try to redeem the lofty with a
> diabolical reversal: through the acceptance of the base . . . this is
> what we cannot and must not have.
>
> Umberto Eco, *The Name of the Rose*

Umberto Eco's novel imagines a book on comedy, Aristotle's lost sequel to *Poetics*. The book is at the heart of a monastic conspiracy to keep humour out of religion by suppressing the Aristotelian authority that lends comedy intellectual legitimacy, preventing 'the operation of the belly' becoming 'an operation of the mind' (Eco, 1983: 474). Eco's conspirators fear that if comedy were to be rehabilitated within respectable academic contexts, the conceptual order of things would be radically altered, and with it the social fabric that draws on its hierarchies, as 'on the day when the Philosopher's word would justify the marginal jests of the debauched imagination, or when what has been marginal would leap to the center, every trace of the center would be lost' (Eco, 1983: 475). To preserve the status quo, the book is infused with a poison that kills all who read it.

While Eco's conspiracy is entirely fictional, it is the case that comedy has been denigrated in the academy, especially in comparison with tragedy, due in part to the absence of an important treatment of it in the Classical tradition. Comedy is often perceived as ephemeral and lacking intellectual weight, or, in the protests of those who claim that explaining a joke kills it or that things are 'just' for laughs, is seen as an aspect of communication that is emphatically closed to study and interrogation. While there are a number of reasons for the cultural second-place that comedy occupies, the most forceful among them are a product of concepts relating to the nature of literature, the proper objects for intellectual enquiry, and rejection of supposedly 'popular' forms in favour of elite ones. While earlier writers like Congreve and Meredith had stood up for the corrective merits of comedy, it is only in the twentieth century that we meet critics who are prepared to 'redeem' it as a culturally rich and critically significant form within a rigorous intellectual context. This chapter will consider some of the reasons for the place of comedy in the academy, and the work of some of its most important critics.

PLATO AND ARISTOTLE

The generic codification of drama in Ancient Greece laid the foundations for the subsequent disparagement of comedy in relation to tragedy. In Hellenic philosophy, comedy was thought to belong to the lower human instincts, and, as such, was to be avoided by the man of reason; comedy was a measure against which a rational identity could be formulated. The contaminating qualities of comedy are first asserted in Plato's *Republic* (*c.*370 BC):

> If there are amusing things which you'd be ashamed to do yourself, but which give you a great deal of pleasure when you see them in a comic representation or hear about them in private company – when you don't find them loathsome or repulsive – then isn't this exactly the same kind of behaviour as we uncovered when talking about feeling sad? There's a part of you which wants to make people laugh, but your reason restrains it, because you're afraid of being thought a vulgar clown. Nevertheless, you let it have its way on those other occasions, and you don't realize that the almost inevitable result

of giving it energy in this other context is that you become a comedian in your own life.

(Plato, 1994: 360)

Here Plato establishes an historically dogged distinction that opposes the vulgarity of laughter and clowning to the sovereignty of reason. The comic is believed to exist outside of the subject rather than be a quality residing within him or her, leading to a conception of the human subject as an essentially serious creature for whom the comic is a temporary identity that may be encountered on occasion. Prolonged exposure to comic thoughts or performances can result in the debased transformation of the subject into a comedian, as we 'irrigate and tend to those things when they should be left to wither, and . . . [make] them our rulers when they should be our subjects' (Plato, 1994: 360). Plato's denigration of comedy in *Republic* exists within the context of a broader project to categorize and index subjectivity for the purposes of cultivating the ideal person in the ideal state. Unhealthy or counterproductive thoughts, emotions, and behaviours are restrained by an act of will and reason is promoted above all other things.

The generic distinctions that Aristotle lays out in his *Poetics* (*c.*330 BC) represent the fundamental pattern through which the opposition between comedy and tragedy has been understood in literary culture. *Poetics*, the most influential work of literary theory in Western culture, implicitly establishes the idea that comedy is a type of drama, with specific rules, character types, and outcomes. Both comedy and tragedy, Aristotle argues, seek to represent the world mimetically, but whereas tragedy 'is an imitation of an action that is admirable, complete and possesses magnitude' (Aristotle, 1996: 10) set in the world of people of substance, comedy deals with people who are 'low' by nature:

Comedy is (as we have said) an imitation of inferior people – not, however, with respect to every kind of defect: the laughable is a species of what is disgraceful. The laughable is an error or disgrace that does not involve pain or destruction: for example, a comic mask is ugly and distorted, but does not involve pain.

(Aristotle, 1996: 9)

Aristotle's laws of narrative distinction contain unambiguous value judgements that echo Plato's. His comedy is a non-violent form conceived primarily in terms of derogation: inferiority, 'error', and 'disgrace'. Comedy is an imitation of the ridiculous or unworthy aspects of human behaviour, where little of real significance passes on stage and 'inferiority' amounts to a failure to uphold moral virtues. Ideally, tragedy depicts the decline in fortune of an individual which 'is not due to any moral defect or depravity, but to an error of some kind' that inevitably leads to a death or to the experience of 'something terrible' (Aristotle, 1996: 21). Comedy, on the other hand, ends happily and conflicts are resolved: 'In comedy even people who are the bitterest enemies in the story . . . go off reconciled in the end, and no one gets killed by anybody' (Aristotle, 1996: 22). The brief discussion of comedy in *Poetics* is not intended as a dismissal, but as a counterpoint to tragedy in the contrast between genres, the one form representing 'high' ideals, the other 'low', for the purposes of producing a symmetrical literary system that reflects a conception of humanity as an amalgamation of two competing facets of character. It is widely assumed that Aristotle intended, or had already written, a companion volume that concentrated on comedy, but this text, if it ever existed, is now lost. A brief document entitled the *Tractatus Coisilinianus*, which outlines the construction of jokes and catalogues types of comic characters, may offer an insight into its content; but its own provenance is uncertain, being 'variously hailed as the key to Aristotle's views on comedy and denounced as a sorry Byzantine fabrication' (Janko, 1984: 1). To what extent the existence of a comic *Poetics* would have improved the reputation of comedy in academic or scholarly circles it is impossible to speculate, yet given the centrality of Aristotle to the history of ideas, his implied validation through an extended treatise would have undoubtedly improved its standing. But the most important factor in deciding the status of comedy in the academy is the simple fact that as tragedy occupies the privileged space in *Poetics*, it has been seen to occupy the privileged space in literary culture. The influence of Aristotle's brief remarks on the shape of generic thinking are difficult to overstate: 'On this Aristotelian basis', writes M. S. Silk, ' . . . all subsequent Western theory has been founded, most explicitly in the shape of a series of syntheses, late Greek, Graeco-Roman or Renaissance, but explicitly or implicitly in all ages' (Silk, 2000: 54).

GENRE TROUBLE

As comedy is a diffuse term, so its place within academic scholarship has often been confused, even while its generic boundaries were at one time extremely rigid. The Roman comedy of Plautus (*c.*254–184 BC) and Terence (*c.*190 or 180–159 BC), known as 'New Comedy' and composed of a body of only twenty-six plays that were adaptations of Greek originals, was built almost exclusively on plots and characters so similar that to modern readers the genre seems narrow and formulaic. From another perspective, however, it tells us that the concept of comedy was well defined, and that the form was specific, coherent, and specialized at this time. The demarcations of comedy would never be so clear again. During the medieval period, the identity of comedy became confused and its boundaries blurred. Drama that conformed to Aristotle's formulae or directly emulated the writers of classical antiquity disappeared from literary culture with the fall of the Roman Empire and the degradation of the theatres, not to re-emerge until the fifteenth century. Generations of medieval grammarians did keep Aristotle's definitions alive alongside the texts of plays by Greek and Roman authors, and the distinction between comedy and tragedy was upheld in commentaries and treatises by writers such as Diomedes, Evanthius, and Donatus. But while these authors continued to transmit Hellenic ideas about comedy, they had little or no first-hand experience of what they were writing about. As a result, the classical definition of comedy maintained in scholarship had little bearing on comedic practice.

In the medieval period, comedy, previously conceived solely as drama, began to appear in both prose and verse as a distinguishable mode or tone rather than a technically rigid genre. As Paul G. Ruggiers writes, 'the forms of tragedy and comedy inherited from classical antiquity had no real impact upon the like modes of experience . . . in the Middle Ages', resulting in considerable diversity and discontinuity amongst comic forms (Ruggiers 1977: 7; Shanzer, 2002: 25). Amongst other things, there developed alternative prose types to which 'were attached the considerations of their serious and non-serious biases, and of the subject matter and vocabulary once reserved for the dramatic forms, but now applied inadvertently to the narrative fictions' (Ruggiers 1977: 7). This is the ultimate source of the problems of definition and confusion that inevitably arise in discussions of comedy – when 'comedy' can describe at once a dramatic genre, a literary mode, or instances of humour real or fictional. Both Boccaccio (1313–75) and Chaucer (c.1343–1400) were interested in the textures and possibilities of comedy and tragedy, yet neither was a dramatist. The clearest example of the broadening of the term in the medieval period is the title of Dante's *Divine Comedy* (begun c.1314), a poem that contains little that may be described as humorous. Structurally, however, Dante's poem, like Greek and Roman comedy before it, moves out of ignorance to understanding and towards a happy conclusion, or in terms of its theological framework, from despair to eternal life. In a letter to his friend Can Grande, Dante further explains his choice of title by indicating that it is written in what he calls 'an unstudied and low style' (Dante, 1984: 31). Medieval mystery and morality plays similarly incorporated comic elements in accordance with these principles, 'comedy' representing a condition of ignorance prior to eventual salvation. The Vice figure of the drama was often intentionally humorous, an inversion of the ideal qualities of humanity presented in the didacticism of the principal narrative.

With the rise of Humanism, the renaissance educational movement that devoted itself to the study of classical authors and the pursuit of pure literary style, Aristotelian standards of generic difference were reintroduced to literature. Humanist scholars returned to their sources in Greek and Roman texts, the reputation of these volumes having flourished since the fall of Constantinople in 1453 and the reintroduction of otherwise overlooked authors it occasioned in Western Europe, and sought to emulate their language, plots, and structures. Nicholas Udall's *Ralph Roister Doister* (1552), for example, widely recognized as the first comic drama in English, proudly proclaimed its classical heritage:

> The wyse poets long time heretofore,
> Under merrie Comedies secretes did declare,
> Wherein was contained very virtuous lore,
> With mysteries and forewarnings very rare.
> Such to write neither Plautus nor Terence dyd spare,
> Which among the learned at this day beares the bell;
> These with such other therein dyd excel.
>
> (Udall, 1984: Prologue, ll. 15–21)

Udall, headmaster at Eton, saw his play as an anglicized Latin comedy, affording it both academic and moral integrity. When, in 1588, Maurice Kyffin translated Terence's *Andria* in a version principally to be used in schools, he prefaced the text with praise of Terence's style, clearly revealing the influence of the comic theory of Donatus:

> Among all the Romane writers, there is none (by the judgement of the learned) so much available to be read and studied, for the true knowledge and purity of the Latin tong, as *Pub. Terentius*: for, sith the cheefest matter in speech, is to speak properly and aptly, and that we have not a more conning Craft-master of apt and proper speech than Terence, well worthy is he then, even will all ease and diligence, to be both taught and learned before any other.
>
> (Kyffin, 1588: sig. A1, recto)

As early modern scholarship favoured classical models for the purity of their form and style, Sir Philip Sidney, in his *Defence of Poetry* (1579–80), complained of the disregard theatre practitioners had for generic boundaries, particularly taking them to task for their

> Gross absurdities, how all their plays be neither right tragedies, nor right comedies, mingling kings and clowns, not because the matter so carrieth it, but thrust in the clown by head and shoulders to play a part in majestical matters with neither decency nor discretion, so as neither the admiration and commiseration, nor the right sportfulness, is by their mongrel tragic-comedy obtained.
>
> (Sidney, 1991: 67)

Sidney's exasperation with mixed modes stems from a desire to impose conformity on the drama of the Elizabethan stage, and to lend it some gravity. Yet, as Stephen Orgel tells us, comedy was not 'simply the opposite of tragedy, but . . . the largest condition of drama' during this period (Orgel, 1994: 36). There is some anecdotal evidence that the comic aspects of renaissance drama may have been amongst the most prominent for contemporary audiences. London doctor and astrologer Simon Forman, for example, records his presence at a performance of *The Winter's Tale* on 15 May 1611. His report differs considerably from modern readings of the play as it concentrates almost exclusively on the clown character of Autolycus, which leads him to conclude that the play is about 'feigned beggars or fawning fellows' (Rowse, 1976: 310). Similarly, the Swiss tourist Thomas Platter, in the playhouse for a performance of Shakespeare's *Julius Caesar* at the Globe in 1599, mentions little about the tragedy aside the dance that followed it, which was performed 'exceedingly gracefully, according to their custom, two in each group dressed in men's and two in women's apparel' (quoted in Shakespeare, 1998: 1).

Throughout the medieval and renaissance periods, therefore, it seems that a scholarly definition of comedy, loyal to the Aristotelian blueprint, existed separately from popular plays, poems, and other vehicles for humour. The academy's apparent distance from popular culture is confirmed in the nineteenth and twentieth centuries and is concomitant with the rise of professional English literary studies. Inspired by the Victorian poet and critic Matthew Arnold (1822–88), and largely concerned with what Chris Baldick calls 'questions of literature's social function' (Baldick, 1987: 18), the view of comedy in the universities at this time is best summed up by a footnote in F. R. Leavis's study of the novel, *The Great Tradition* (1948), that calls the work of eighteenth-century satirist Laurence Sterne 'irresponsible', 'nasty', and 'trifling' (Leavis, 1972: 10). As Baldick says elsewhere, critical opinion held that 'the author's quality of mind [was] reflected in the quality of the literary work: to speak of the maturity or integrity of one is to commend the other' (Baldick, 1996: 164). Comic themes were thought to be local and vulgar, antithetical to a vision of art that believed in its ability to communicate beyond the moment of its creation like tragedy. A passage from A. C. Bradley's prestigious British Academy lecture of 1912 expresses this idea. 'Most of the great tragedies', he writes,

> leave a certain imaginative impression of the highest value. . . . What we witness is not the passion and doom of mere individuals. The forces that meet in tragedy stretch far beyond the little group of figures and the tiny tract of space and time in which they appear. The darkness that covers the scene, and the light that strikes across it, are more than our common night and day.
>
> (Bradley, 1929: 75)

The literary establishment view was that comedy did not belong in such cultured and profound company, and that 'Comedy and satire should be kept in their proper place, like the moral standards and social classes which they symbolize' (Frye, 1990: 22).

FERTILITY AND THE '*ÉLAN VITAL*': CORNFORD, BERGSON, LANGER

'The history of literary criticism is also the history of attempts to make an honest creature, as it were, of comedy', writes David Daniell (Daniell 1997: 102). The first significant modern attempt to make comedy a 'serious' object of study appeared in 1914, written by a scholar of Ancient Greece. Francis Macdonald Cornford's *The Origin of Attic Comedy* is a combination of literary criticism and anthropology that attempts to reconstruct the sources and forms of the original comic entertainments. Cornford was part of a Cambridge-based movement of anthropological classicists, and *The Origin of Attic Comedy*, like James George Frazer's enormous anthropological survey *The Golden Bough* (1890–1915), is part of a broader school of Edwardian scholarship that examined the ceremonies and beliefs of primitive communities in an effort to see their influence on modern thinking and social organization. Cornford's text looks in detail at the structure of Greek Old Comedy, especially that of Aristophanes, and demonstrates its ceremonial roots and the relationship of its characters to significant elements of seasonal rituals. Cornford argues for an aboriginal relationship between comedy and the religiously sanctioned revel and fertility beliefs that stemmed from Dionysial and Phallic ritual (Cornford, 1914: 3). The study describes how agrarian rituals, beginning with simple work-chants and songs, developed in form and complexity until they had become invested with significance that led to prepared and stylized activities growing up around them. A character-istic ritual of this type was the phallic procession, a parade of phallic symbols that used profanity and sexual and scatological imagery as a kind of benevolent magic to protect the community. As he writes,

> Besides the distribution of benign influence . . . these processions have also the converse magical intent of defeating and driving away bad

influences of every kind. The phallus itself is no less a negative charm against evil spirits than a positive agent of fertilisation. But the simplest of all methods of expelling malign influences of any kind is to abuse them with the most violent language. . . . There can be no doubt that the element of invective and personal satire which distinguishes the Old Comedy is directly descended from the magical abuse of the phallic procession, just as its obscenity is due to sexual magic.

(Cornford, 1914: 49–50)

Through a process of historical accretion and growth, ceremonies of this kind become formulaic, developing into a symbolic dialogue, or *agon*, from which emerged drama. Comedy was now an identifiable form that retained its characteristics from ancient folk practices long after the beliefs that nurtured them had either become obsolete or been subsumed into the secular aspects of the performance. While the exact nature of this transformation is not entirely clear, Cornford argues that the reason that the forms of the fertility songs and dances were preserved after their religious significance had evaporated was because they were, essentially, funny:

The . . . double intent of stimulating fertility and averting bad influences lies at the root of many forms of festival dance, which, when the serious purpose has died out of them, are kept under the sanction of old customs, and partly for the sake of pleasurable obscenity.

(Cornford, 1914: 50)

Comedy now had well-defined structural components: the *agon*, in which the hero-protagonist struggles with an adversary and wins; the enjoyment of the victory, celebrated by feast and sacrifice, and a final victory procession, the *komos*, followed by marriage or some kind of resurrection. The relationship of comedy to agrarian fertility rituals is most clearly seen in Aristophanes' play *The Acharnians* (425 BC), the oldest comedy in existence. Having been drinking, the farmer Dikaiopolis mounts a phallus on a pole and celebrates his 'Country Dionysia' by making offerings of cake and asking the god to bless his sexual adventures with the neighbour's slave: 'For now is the time to be merry, with pleasure for one and / all' (Aristophanes, 1973: 61). Comedy, then, is a secularized version of a ritual that was so entertaining that it could not be allowed to die out.

The methodological impulse of Cornford's text, a return to ritualistic sources and an examination of the cultural significance of the comic, was representative of a new departure in modern academic treatments of comedy. Studies of this kind give comedy a credibility that it did not possess in the qualitative analyses and exclusions of English Literature departments. It also had the benefit of providing it with the best classical ancestry. Cornford's study was also a product of its time, as for all its experimentalism, the literary culture of modernism was simultaneously fascinated by the distant myths of pre-Christian Europe. The fundamental identity of the people was a compelling issue in the first half of the twentieth century, and the compilation and analysis of myth fuelled a popular or 'folk' image of the past. Perhaps this was an attempt at finding roots in an otherwise alienating modern world, but its implications are wider. Its symptoms appear all over modernist literature; for example, the high visibility of both *The Golden Bough* and Jessie Weston's *From Ritual to Romance* in the footnotes of T. S. Eliot's *The Waste Land* (1922) indicates that the themes of modern fragmentation in the poem hope to find anchors in the mythic past. In Britain, there was concern that colonizing the world meant losing a sense of self. Anxiety about the loss of indigenous culture was reflected in, for example, the founding of institutions such as Cecil Sharp's English Folk Dance Society in 1911, which began its work collecting songs and dances from a provincial and predominantly oral tradition. Comedy, understood in these terms, is an authentic, continuous expression of the communal identity as it encounters the life force.

The philosophy of Henri Bergson (1859–1941) has been influential in conceiving of comedy as a manifestation of vitality. Central to Bergson's thought were the dynamic forces of intuition and impulse, the '*élan vital*', creative and demanding life forces that reveal themselves to us continually and through which all social interaction is mediated. Bergson's famous essay 'Laughter' (1900), discussed in further detail in Chapter 6, claims that humour is born in moments when the life force is momentarily usurped or eclipsed by an involuntary manifestation of automatism or reduction of the body to a lifeless machine. The fullest articulation of comedy as vitalism appears in Susanne Langer's study of aesthetics, *Feeling and Form*, which also calls Bergson 'pre-eminently the artists' philosopher' (Langer, 1953: 114). For Langer, art is an intuitive and essentially creative process driven by the need to be alive. Comedy is:

> an art form that arises naturally wherever people are gathered to celebrate life, in spring festivals, triumphs, birthdays, weddings, or initiations. For it expresses the elementary strains and resolutions of animate nature, the animal drives that persist even in human nature, the delight man takes in his special mental gifts that make him the lord of creation; it is an image of human vitality holding its own in the world amid the surprises of unplanned coincidence.
>
> (Langer, 1953: 331)

This version of the comic exists in the routine obscenity surrounding marriage celebrations, in the jubilant nicknaming of genitalia, or in bouts of celebratory drinking that follow a triumph, however minor. What is important, emphasizes Langer, is that the comic spirit constitutes an essential element of being human and, more importantly, being alive. This definition is complicated by the very full tradition of black humour that exists in Western culture, and which is prevalent in both literature and social interaction. Jokes about death or the fear of death can be devastatingly funny, but do not seem to conform to Langer's model unless morbid reflection itself constitutes a triumphant acknowledgement that one is still breathing. What is important about the work of Bergson and Langer is that it positions comedy at the ontological centre. In claiming for comedy a close relationship to fertility ritual, rites of passage, and reproductive events, these writers reintroduced comedy into the academic mainstream as a genre in which the fundamental imprint of human existence is as evident as in its tragic counterpart. However, in doing so they also reproduced the terms of the argument that elevated tragedy and denigrated comedy: even though comedy has been shown to be an object worthy of significant study, it is simultaneously shown to be closer to nature than art, and closer, therefore, to the body than the soul.

SPRINGTIME AND FESTIVAL: FRYE AND BARBER

It is no accident that literary studies devoted to the study of comedy should appear first in areas that are unquestionably perceived as belonging to 'high culture', as if their association with culturally central concepts would protect them from accusations of low-mindedness. The trope of comedy as life force is particularly evident in Shakespeare studies, much of it indebted to the distinguished work of the Canadian scholar Northrop Frye (1906–91), who saw in Shakespearean comedy a spirit of regeneration in sympathy with the natural rhythm of the seasons. Basing itself on a series of archetypal structures in harmony with the four seasons of the year, Frye's *The Anatomy of Criticism* (1957) offers the idea that 'the fundamental form of [mythical] process is cyclical movement, the alternation of success and decline, effort and relapse, life and death' (Frye, 1990: 158). Humanity, in other words, creates an imaginatively inhabitable world of literary fiction carved from the patterns of life and death that assimilates the idea of seasonal rejuvenation into narrative. This is the case especially with narrative produced prior to the advent of modernity and the demythologization of culture that accompanied it. Narrative patterns, writes Frye,

> are usually divided into four main phases, the four seasons of the year being the type for four periods of the day (morning, noon, evening, night), four aspects of the water-cycle (rain, fountains, rivers, sea or snow), four periods of life (youth, maturity, age, death) and the like.
>
> (Frye, 1990: 160)

From these archetypes are formed 'narrative categories of literature broader than, or logically prior to, the ordinary literary genres', meta-generic forms from which more specific genres are derived: 'the romantic, the tragic, the comic, and the ironic and the satiric' (Frye, 1990: 162). These pre-generic 'moods' of narrative have in turn strong associative connections with the texture of the seasons: summer for romance, autumn for tragedy, winter for irony and satire, and spring for comedy.

Spring, the transitional season between hardship and repose, is placed perfectly to enact the theme of rebirth and the battle of winter and summer that is the dominant analytical metaphor in Frye's theory of comedy.

Shakespeare's comedy, he says, 'is the drama of the green-world, its plot being assimilated to the ritual themes of the triumph of life and love over the waste land' (Frye, 1990: 182). The 'green world' is a phrase widely taken up by Shakespeare criticism as it offers a convincing template for the symbolism of the narrative structure of his comedy. 'Green worlds' are wish fulfilment locations, always rural, often enchanted, in which the normal business of the town is suspended and the pleasurable pastimes of holiday prevail. Shakespearean green worlds include the wood outside Athens in *A Midsummer Night's Dream*, the coast of Illyria in *Twelfth Night* (1601–02), Portia's Belmont in *The Merchant of Venice* (1596–97), and the Forest of Arden in *As You Like It* (1599). Associated with love, leisure, levelled social hierarchy, and play, the green world serves as a space in which solutions to urban problems can be worked through. As court or city rules no longer apply, gender distinctions can be disregarded, the mythical and the quotidian can intermingle, and drunks and braggarts are able to live freely away from the tyranny of work or the regime of the clock. In order to solve the problems of the town, represented by a 'blocking agent', usually a father figure or envoy of the older generation whose blind insistence on his authority forbids the success of relationships founded on love, society must be divested of its most fundamental suppositions, such as the nature of law, or the relationship between the sexes, in order that those suppositions may be reconstructed in the form of a happy ending. Immersion in the green world is immeasurably healing, but always temporary; holiday is defined only as such because it must be distinguished from the everyday world. In the narrative of *As You Like It*, says Frye, Rosalind is the representative of spring, inspiring renewal in the dormant inhabitants of Arden and ultimately triumphing over the cruel and unforgiving winter of Duke Frederick. Through her intervention, made possible by her entry into the forest, the unlawfully usurped Duke Senior is reinstated, reconciliations are brought about, and, after a round of divinely sponsored weddings, society is rejuvenated with the promise of a new ruling generation and their heirs.

Frye's account is both convincing and symmetrically satisfying, but it brings with it two key objections. The first is the extent to which comedic structure is privileged over content, the degree that his discussion of varied and distinct plays can become a list of titles whose similarity rests on their final reconciliations. This is a shortcoming of all structuralist and narratological critical practices, and in mitigation it should be noted that Frye's project aims to study structural similarities and not offer close readings of individual texts. However, through the reduction to narrative units, literary difference is lost through the absorption into a homogenized structural model. A recurrent problem of comedy criticism is its focus on structure and plot over character and dialogue, a result of both the critical prejudice that tragic heroes are individuals, and the practice of writing comic ones as types. The second objection would be the extent to which a large part of *The Anatomy of Criticism* depends on our acceptance of Frye's overall thesis that literary forms, at least in the originary phases of their development, mirror the procession of the seasons in what amounts to a grossly extended pathetic fallacy. Does all literature conform in tone to the overbearing influence of four seasons? Are all writers informed by an unconscious force that imposes itself on their work through an enigmatic process of arboreal ventriloquism? Is it entirely inconceivable that a narrative could be constructed and read outside those terms?

Another influential Shakespearean, C. L. Barber, believed that structural readings of literature failed to grasp the truth of art. In his *Shakespeare's Festive Comedy* (1959), he indirectly challenges Frye with an accusation of insensitivity, writing that, 'No figure in the carpet is the carpet. There is in the pointing out of patterns something that is opposed to life and art, an ungraciousness which artists in particular feel and resent' (Barber, 1963: 4). For Barber, literature is full of moments of 'design beyond design' that possess a vitality that resonates much further than the generic and narrative structures in which they are placed. Barber's intention, and the nature of his contribution to the understanding of comedy, was to demonstrate the relevance of the Elizabethan social practice of holiday festivities that inform comedy and are reflected in it. This is a sixteenth-century remodelling of *The Origin of Attic Comedy*, privileging an historicist methodology that holds an understanding of original context above other means of reading a literary text. The practices he invokes include festivals like 'the celebration of a marriage, the village wassail or wake . . . Candlemas, Shrove Tuesday, Hocktide, May Day, Whitsuntide, Midsummer Eve, Harvest-home, Halloween and the twelve days of Christmas season ending with Twelfth Night' (Barber, 1963: 5). Such holidays provide the basis for the staged folly, disguise, and masquerade of any number of Shakespeare's plays. For Barber, comedy is essentially 'saturnalian', an experience of pleasurable merrymaking and social inversion named after the revels devoted to the Roman god Saturn. Saturnalian comedy is neither satirical nor political, but devoted to a process Barber calls 'release and clarification'. 'Release' refers to the loosening of social controls during holidays, and leads Barber, like Freud, to ascribe comic pleasure to the redistribution of mental energy normally devoted to social conformity, so that 'the energy normally occupied in maintaining inhibitions is freed for celebration' (Barber, 1963: 7). 'Clarification' is comedy's ability to reaffirm the positive relationship of humanity to its environment, 'a heightened relationship between man and "nature"' (Barber, 1963: 8). Comedy thereby has the dual function of celebrating human relationships and merrymaking, while mocking what it considers 'unnatural', baiting killjoys and miserly characters who fail to observe the feast or show some perverse aversion to happiness. From this perspective, Barber reads a character like Shylock from *The Merchant of Venice* as a representative of anti-festival, a usurer whose anxiety about money stands in joyless contrast to the Venetian Christians who use money 'graciously to live together in a humanly knit group' (Barber, 1963: 167). As the defeat of outsiders and the chastisement of scapegoats is a significant aspect of the comic celebration of communal identity and its life experience, the vilification and forcible conversion of Shylock reveal him as a representative of egregious heterogeneity that must be made to conform to 'healthy' community values. However, Barber's insistence on holiday forms, while not absolute in his discussion of *The Merchant of Venice*, has the effect of naturalizing folk practices and eliding the politics of race that speak through them.

CARNIVAL AND THE MARKETPLACE: BAKHTIN AND THE NEW HISTORICISM

With the re-emergence and dominance of forms of historicism in literary studies in the 1980s and 1990s, the work of one commentator, Mikhail Bakhtin (1895–1975), has been extremely influential. Bakhtin, a Russian formalist who first began working on a theory of the novel after the Russian Revolution, made a major contribution to comedy studies with the monograph *Rabelais and his World*, written as a doctoral dissertation sometime in the later 1930s and unpublished in English until 1968.

Through an analysis of the early modern French comic novelist François Rabelais (*c*.1494–*c*.1553), Bakhtin argues for the existence of two synchronous but contradictory world views during the medieval period. 'Official' culture, which he characterizes as ecclesiastical, sombre, excluding profanity, and suppressing the body, driven by the bureaucracy of the Church and the administration of Grace, is contrasted with what he calls the culture of the marketplace, the popular and boisterous voice of the people. The marketplace is a totemic location for Bakhtin, and one that has certain parallels with the rituals discussed by Cornford and the spontaneous expressions of vitality explored by Langer. 'This territory', writes Bakhtin,

> was a peculiar second world within the official medieval world order and was ruled by a special type of relationship. Officially the palaces, churches, institutions, and private homes were dominated by hierarchy and etiquette, but in the marketplace a special kind of language was heard, almost a language of its own, quite unlike the language of the Church, palace, courts, and institutions.
>
> (Bakhtin, 1984: 154)

The language of the marketplace is the idiom of the plebeian classes, the expression of 'natural' feeling, coarse, unlettered, and unmediated by the expectations of formality. This is a vision of culture at ease with, and making fun of, graphic descriptions of sexual activity and bodily functions, ridiculing officials and officialdom, and violating officially designated rules of etiquette and decorum. The world of the marketplace operates according to what is essentially a comic logic, one that runs parallel to official, serious, improving culture, laughing at it, and sometimes violently humiliating it.

Bakhtin's most important contribution to later analyses of comedy is his theory of carnival. He argues that carnival is the vehicle of an authentic proletarian voice answering the ascetic oppressions of the ruling classes. Carnival, literally 'a putting away of meat', is the period immediately before Lent, the Christian phase of abstinence that takes place over forty days in February and March and concludes on Easter Sunday. Carnival takes place on Shrove Tuesday, the day before Lent begins. In French-speaking countries, carnival is called '*Mardi Gras*', or fat Tuesday, helpfully signifying the sensual indulgence and misrule that comes before the Lenten fast. As a fixture of the medieval calendar, carnival was a special holiday that permitted the temporary suspension of social rules and codes of conduct and deference. The Flemish artist Peter Bruegel's painting of a popular medieval and early modern theme, *The Battle of Carnival and Lent* (1559), presents Carnival as a gorged, corpulent, and self-indulgent figure, engaged in an endless contest with gaunt Lenten piety. In Bakhtin's work, this contest is more than an embodiment of the eternal struggle between the flesh and the spirit but a manifestation of popular opposition to the dominant order and the enactment of alternative regimes:

> As opposed to the official feast, one might say that carnival celebrated temporary liberation from the prevailing truth and from the established order; it marked the suspension of all hierarchical rank, privileges, norms and prohibitions. Carnival was the true feast of time, the feast of becoming, change and renewal. It was hostile to all that was immortalized and completed.
>
> (Bakhtin, 1984: 10)

The inversions and suspensions permitted and legitimized by carnival represent substantive challenges to authority, therefore offering the possibility that comedy, invested with the spirit of festive and carnival traditions, may also be an expression of popular discontent. Some critics have seen in Bakhtin's work an almost utopian view of medieval culture that is more akin to wish fulfilment than historical research. Aaron Gurevich, for example, questions whether or not Bakhtin had not 'transposed some aspects of contemporary life in Stalinist Russia into the epoch' he was dealing with (Gurevich, 1997: 58).

Recent historicist and some poststructuralist critics have found Bakhtin's theory of opposing cultures particularly productive. Such criticism is drawn to comedy via its thematization of misrule and the visibility of characters from the lower social ranks. Perhaps the most influential critical position of this kind is new historicism, a methodology that came to prominence in the 1980s, and whose practice is best summed up by Steven Mullaney, who writes that, 'literary criticism is conceived not as an end in itself, but as a vehicle, a means of gaining access to tensions and contradictions less clearly articulated in other social forums but all the more powerful for their partial occlusion' (Mullaney, 1988: x). With this in mind, new historicism reads comedy as a potential site of social disruption, using the comic as a medium for the message of dissent. However, according to new historicist formulations of the configuration of state power, it is a medium that is simultaneously monitored and controlled by the authorities that it seeks to subvert. As Stephen Greenblatt writes of Shakespearean drama in his essay 'Invisible Bullets': during the process of transgression and inversion, 'authority is subjected to open, sustained and radical questioning before it is reaffirmed, with ironic reservations, at the close' (Greenblatt, 1985: 29). Power absorbs the potential for change, permitting itself to be questioned for the tactical and pragmatic purposes of seeming to appear open, before finally reasserting itself once more: 'Within this theatrical setting, there is a remarkable insistence upon the paradoxes, ambiguities, and tensions of authority, but this apparent production of subversion is . . . the very condition of power' (Greenblatt, 1985: 44–45). Inversion and misrule, then, exist within a matrix of 'licensed transgression', and are expedient outlets for reckless behaviour that enable the continuance of the social order. As Olivia remarks of Feste, the representative of festival in *Twelfth Night*, 'There is no slander / in an allowed fool' (Shakespeare, 1989: 1.5.88–89). Greenblatt assesses the potential of comedy to cause social upset in the following terms:

> It is precisely because of the English form of absolutist theatricality that Shakespeare's drama, written for a theatre subject to state censorship, can be so relentlessly subversive: the form itself, as a primary expression of Renaissance power, helps to contain the radical doubts it continually evokes.
>
> (Greenblatt, 1985: 45)

An absolutist monarchical message is effectively reinforced and validated through the dramatization of objections and subversions of it. Passages which are seemingly transgressive or dissenting are permitted on account of their ultimate defeat and containment within the form. Any potential for offence must have been countered by the message of monarchical status quo, otherwise, Greenblatt argues, the Master of the Revels, the official dramatic censor, would have erased them and punished their author. How convincing, however, is this concept of the 'big brother' state that permits objection only that it might enforce itself at a much more insidious level? Certainly, comedy was subject to censorship in the early modern period. We know that the *Henry IV* plays had been modified by such an intervention, as the character of Sir John Oldcastle, a Lollard martyr and member of the powerful Cobham family, had to be renamed Sir John Falstaff to appease his offended descendents. Ben Jonson, along with his collaborators, was imprisoned in 1597 and the theatres made to submit to an enforced closure due to the outrage caused by their satirical play *The Isle of Dogs*, now lost. But the question is whether or not the form invariably renders any potentially political content safe. As Janet Clare states in her study of censorship on the early modern stage, the Master of the Revels could be both inconsistent and arbitrary, which presumably allowed some satire through unaltered (Clare, 1990: 122). Greenblatt's absolutist model, however, suggests that power has comprehensive coverage, is co-ordinated and efficient at every level, and immune to mistakes and oversights.

Peter Stallybrass and Allon White's *The Politics and Poetics of Transgression* (1986) offers an alternative view. This is a radical materialist reading of Bakhtin that can be said to have rescued some of his ideas from the romanticization of the marketplace and reformulated them as a more credible political force in which the marginal is understood to be genuinely creative and disruptive. Stallybrass and White see carnival and comic forms addressing 'the social classifications of values, distinction and judgements which underpin practical reason', where carnival 'systematically inverts the relations of subject and object, agent and instrument, husband and wife, old and young, animal and human, master and slave' (Stallybrass and White, 1986: 56). These upheavals reformulate, for a temporary period at least, socially sanctioned power relationships, bringing the margin to the centre, making it visible and giving it voice. This is not to say that carnival is suddenly a politically progressive force, however, as, 'although it re-orders the terms of the binary pair, it cannot alter the terms themselves', as inversion of the terms of normal social operation is not the same as redefining them (Stallybrass and White, 1986: 56). The carnivalesque is not then equipped to topple the dominant order, but neither is the dominant order able to silence the carnivalesque; Stallybrass and White imagine both terms engaged in a mutually dependent but antagonistic relationship, in which each contains an element of its other that it uses to define itself. 'A recurrent pattern emerges', they write,

> the 'top' attempts to reject and eliminate the 'bottom' for reasons of prestige and status, only to discover, not only that it is in some way frequently dependent upon that low-Other . . . but also that the top *includes* that low symbolically, as a primarily eroticised constituent of its own fantasy life.
>
> (Stallybrass and White, 1986: 7)

Comic inversion not only makes visible those excluded from the hierarchy, therefore, but also symbolically foregrounds the tensions and desires that are elided parts of the identity of power itself, revealing power not to be the coherent and all-pervasive monolith of new historicism, but constituted of contradictions and unacknowledged dependencies.

A further challenge to the critical tendency to reduce dissent to collusion in support of the absolutist tactics of the state appears in Michael Bristol's *Carnival and Theater* (1985). Bristol takes issue with the new historicism's conception of power as 'always singular, a unity and also a plenitude', as it means it would be 'necessary for festivals to be completely unselfconscious occasions in which nothing was ever learned, and for the participants to cooperate, year after year, in an oppressive routine contrary to their interests' (Bristol, 1985: 15, 27). Finding the containment model of power unsubtle and unrealistic, he invokes the work of anthropologist Victor Turner to understand the relationship between carnival and authority. Turner makes a distinction between types of festive activity that are 'liminal' and those that are 'liminoid'. 'Liminal' phenomena are those carnival or festive activities that remain bound by their archaic form to the extent that they are simply the residue of a previously significant ritual or the repetition of an inversion that remains entirely unanalysed by its participants. An example of this might be the erection of a maypole or performance of a morris dance in a modern town. 'Liminoid' activities, however, are 'not merely reversive, they are often subversive, representing radical critiques of the central structure and proposing alternative models' (Bristol, 1985: 38). Liminoid activities, then, contain the elements of genuine social commentary and conflict, and can extend the definition of festivity to include theatrical performances and riots. Rather than being contained by an authority that tacitly permits festive outbursts,

> Popular festive form reminds the ruling elite that they may actually rule relatively incompletely and ineffectively. Much of the conduct of everyday life, and many of the details of political and economic practice, proceed quite independently of the wishes of the power structure. Carnival is an heuristic instrument of considerable scope and flexibility. Though it is a festive and primarily symbolic activity, it has immediate pragmatic aims, most immediately that of objectifying a collective determination to conserve the authority of the community to set its own standards of behavior and social discipline, and to enforce those standards by appropriate means.
>
> (Bristol, 1985: 52)

Festival is not contained by authority, therefore, but rather overrides it in certain circumstances by asserting local plebeian codes of conduct over the representatives of officialdom. Social practices like the charivari, a cacophonous procession and serenade undertaken by the inhabitants of a village or district for the purposes of deriding and humiliating an unpopular marriage or person, are clearly used as a means of regulating the life of the community outside of official legislation. The humiliation of Malvolio in *Twelfth Night* may serve as an illustration. The gulling of Malvolio and the presentation of him as an extravagant lover 'cross-gartered', is a festive castigation of the sour puritan steward whose very name means 'ill-will'. Sir Toby, Sir Andrew, Feste, and Maria ridicule Malvolio's pretensions to marry the wealthy Olivia, and then continue to torment him until he is perceived to be mad. Festivity therefore pursues authority, which is ridiculous because it is inflexible, and forces it to adapt to the demands of the community.

Comedy's perceived association with a kind of folk politics has therefore given it legitimacy in modern academic discourse. Following Cornford's literary anthropology and reading it through Bakhtin's concept of carnival, comedy becomes useful to academia as a literary counterweight to strict regimes, an expression of a communal life force that inverts the social order and offers short-term liberation from authoritarian pressure. By associating it so clearly with plebeian culture, however, modern critical interest is guilty of retaining the elitist generic divisions that once denigrated comedy, keeping it as the working-class cousin of aristocratic tragedy and other 'serious' forms.

2

COMIC IDENTITY

Two babies were born on the same day at the same hospital. They lay there and looked at each other. Their families came and took them away. Eighty years later, by a bizarre coincidence, they lay in the same hospital, on their deathbeds, next to each other. One of them looked at the other and said, 'So. What did you think?'

Steven Wright

In Woody Allen's film *Zelig* (1983), the title character has a desire to belong so acute that he physically transforms himself into the likeness of whoever he is with. He soon comes to the attention of a baffled medical establishment, and, through the help of a frenzied press that dubs him 'the human chameleon', becomes the biggest celebrity in America. Troops of people are brought to meet him and each time he mimics their appearance, turning into a Rabbi, a 300-pound overeater, an African-American musician, or a Frenchman. While *Zelig* plays with key American issues, most obviously the immigrant experience and the struggle of assimilation, it also focuses a recurrent theme of comedy: the nature and limits of identity. Leonard Zelig is so shy and self-effacing that he is pathologically driven to assume the identities of others. This involves not only absurd physical transformations, but also presents an image of failed interiority, of a man who is a reflective surface. Many comic characters might be said to play on our fears of being incomplete humans through their failures of self-awareness or inability to reflect on the nature of experience. Comic characters are traditionally one-dimensional in the sense that they are apparently unable to learn and change. Bugs Bunny, for example, is madly funny, anarchic, transgressive, and dangerous, and completely incapable of reflecting on his actions. Bugs lives in a perpetual series of excitable nows, changing voice, costume, or tactics within seconds. What makes him funny is the weightlessness of his character, the fact that he is not anchored within an orthodox system of selfhood or responsibility. In Roman New Comedy, character types are so rigidly defined that their behaviours are entirely predictable within given situations. The miser will always be miserly, and the braggart will always boast. In this case, comic identity is derived from a sense of atrophied consciousness. In both examples, human identity is stripped of its subtlety or ambiguity, leaving only monstrous activity. While individual comic characters are infinitely various, it is possible to identify certain features of the categories to which they belong. This chapter will consider the reasoning behind types of comic character, beginning with the most important, distinct personality types.

STEREOTYPES

As we know, traditional comedy is largely plot driven, moving towards ritualistic resolutions such as feasts, marriages, or revelations. Comic characterization is usually subordinate to the demands of plot, and therefore more effectively realized with stereotypes and one-dimensional characters than anything approaching the realistic portrayal of human emotions. A play by Molière, for example, relies on maintaining the tension of the plot rather than the needs of its individuals. Accordingly, we see a seemingly endless parade of characters who are utterly dominated by a single prevalent characteristic, providing the premise for many popular ensemble comedies in which each character reliably acts according to their qualities, such as *The Phil Silvers Show* (1955–59), *Dad's Army* (1968–77), *Are You Being Served?* (1972–85), *The Simpsons* (1989 – present), or the *Carry On* series of films (1958–79). The comedian Mike Myers has said that the principle of single-mindedness is essential to successful comedy, suggesting that 'Comedy characters tend to be a – machine; i.e., Clouseau was a *smug* machine, Pepe Le Pew was a *love* machine, Felix Unger was a *clean* machine, and Austin Powers is a *sex* machine' (quoted in Friend, 2002: 82). Consciously or otherwise, Myers is adapting the Bergsonian view that 'what is essentially laughable is what is done automatically' (Bergson, 1980: 155). Automatism, or the channelling of diverse thoughts and feelings through one overriding principle, has been the impetus behind comic characterization since the New Comedy of the third century BC, and provides us with the set of comic stereotypes that have provided the blueprint for comic characterization from the renaissance to the present.

New Comedy is derived from the work of the Greek dramatist Menander, whose plays, up until the discovery of papyrus fragments in 1905, were known only through the adaptations and embellishments of the Roman comic authors Plautus and Terence. Considering the enormous impact Menander has had on comedy, very little is known about him. He was an Athenian, who according to one account, wrote 108 plays, but had only modest success during his lifetime, and was eclipsed by other authors of New Comedy, of whom even less is known. His standing was completely revised in later antiquity, however, and he was prized for the quality of his plots and the excellence of his characters. Whereas Aristophanic Old Comedy dealt with political institutions, public figures, and fantastical situations, Menandrine New Comedy was concerned with the intimate themes of domestic and private life. New Comedy dramatized the lives of citizens rather than gods and politicians and was interested in romance, sexual desire, the circulation of money, and the imposition of patriarchal order. New Comedy was also the first to conclude with the promise of marriage. Concomitantly, its repertoire of stock characters emerges from the household and orbits around this central domestic space. Menander, Plautus, and Terence populate their plays with variations on the same basic character types: the profligate or impractical young man; the *senex*, or parent; the matronly wife; the *meretrix*, or accomplished courtesan; the clever slave; the nervous parasite; the vulnerable maiden; and the *miles gloriosus*, or swaggering soldier. These characters reflect Menander's absorption of the philosophy of Theophrastus (*c*.370–*c*.288 BC), head of the Peripatetic School after Aristotle, and the author of *Characters*, thirty sketches of human types embodying particular faults and follies. Like stage comedy itself, these amount to possibly the most resilient character types in all Western fiction, with several remaining, in the words of Northrop Frye, 'practically unchanged for twenty-five centuries' (Frye, 1953: 271).

New Comedy is generally considered to be a more conservative form than its Aristophanic predecessor, reflecting a change in the context of Greek drama from the fourth to the third centuries BC. The shift in emphasis from the public arena to life indoors was probably a response to Athens's decreasing political importance, and the fact that its leadership was largely supported by foreign powers, resulting in a loss of the political immediacy that motivated Aristophanes. Audiences may have also changed: as the subsidies which allowed people from all walks of life to attend the theatre disappeared, a more resolutely middle-class audience came to dominate. Their taste, suggests Geoffrey Arnott, was escapist, interested less in the 'recurring disasters of life' and more in stories in which problems 'always resolved in the inevitable happy ending which celebrated and cemented family unity' (quoted in Konstan, 1995: 167). Just as its characterization was formulaic, so were plots, featuring variations on familiar themes. Roman comedy deals repeatedly with the forbidden love of a young man for a prostitute, slave, or otherwise ineligible woman, and the complications of their romance in the face of fierce parental disapproval before finally, through some contortion of the plot, a recognition scene reveals her true identity as a citizen. 'With this device, the conflicting claims of private passion and social responsibility are neatly reconciled, for the waywardness of desire proves to be illusory. The impulse that aspires to the forbidden is domesticated, gratified without danger to public convention, and thus the threat to the city-state ideal of a closed conjugal group is averted' (Konstan, 1983: 24–25). Given that these narratives tend towards the reinforcement of family ties and the maintenance of dynastic status, supporting the privilege of a racially homogenous group in an ethnically diverse empire, stereotypical characterization might be seen as a reassuring ploy that confirms a hegemonic view of the world, and appeals to the comprehensive systems of taxonomy and categorization that existed in Roman intellectual life. As Maurice Charney writes: 'Comic convention postulates a society that is rigidly hierarchical. By the laws of decorum, carefully formulated by such Roman rhetoricians as Cicero and Quintilian, different social classes have their prescribed styles, both of manners and of speech' (Charney, 1978: 51). Representing a range of clearly delineated social types supports a concept of order that asserts its totality by claiming to predict, know, and catalogue the behaviour of all kinds and types of people. Watching a parade of stereotypes, therefore, affords the comfort of confirming an audience's prejudices.

As previously discussed, the reputations of Terence and Plautus were upheld during the medieval and renaissance periods by scholars who valued them primarily as examples of good style. The basic structure of New Comedy had been preserved in the Italian renaissance form known as the *commedia erudita*, or 'learned' comedy, of which Niccolò dei Machiavelli's *La Mandragola* (*c.*1520) is an example. Italian drama has some influence on the structure of English playwriting throughout the 1580s and 1590s, combined with a group of plays known as 'prodigal son' dramas, another fashionable continental model that dramatized the errant ways and eventual reformation of a wayward son. Eventually, these influences came to form city, or 'citizen', comedy, a branch of comic writing devoted to intrigue plots of love and money and the struggle between the older and younger generation amongst the merchant classes of contemporary London. A number of circumstances, including rapid population growth and the emergence of a predominantly capitalist economy over an agrarian one, had raised the visibility of the urban middle classes in England. As a result, these citizens are identified solely with their economic interests, and almost every area of existence is subsumed into their financial dealings, including their sex lives. In city comedy, the slave girl is displaced and the energetic pursuit of the commodity becomes the new object of desire. William Haughton's *Englishmen for My Money* (1598) is generally held to be the first play to fit this description exactly, but it was Ben Jonson (1572–1637), the dramatist who most aggressively asserted his erudition, whose work most clearly exemplified the revived and anglicized Roman form. Jonson believed that comedy was a weapon aimed at the faults, follies, and hypocrisies of the world. The prologue to *The Alchemist* (1610), establishes both his targets and the authorial tone:

> Our *Scene* is *London*, 'cause we would make knowne.
>   No countries mirth is better then our owne,
> No clime breeds better matter, for your whore,
>   Bawd, squire, impostor, many persons more,

> Whose manners, now call'd humours, feed the stage:
>   And which have still beene subject, for the rage
> Or spleene of *comick*-writers.
>> (Jonson, 1979: Prologue, 5–11)

The prologue lists a number of malefactors, and promises the audience a procession of types, 'now call'd humours'. The word 'humour' has its roots in medieval physiognomy, meaning 'moisture' or 'vapour'. Principally employed to describe animal or vegetal fluids, the word came to its present meaning of 'amusement' via the application of medical theory to fictional characterization. Medieval medicine, following Galen (AD 129–99), held that health was regulated by four essential fluids – blood, phlegm, black bile, and choler – existing equally within the human body. When balanced, the humours were complementary and the body enjoyed good health. When disproportionate, and one fluid came to prominence above the others, the body experienced discomfort or disease. From this, it followed that a person's mental qualities, character, and temperament could also be subject to overbearing influences. A preponderance of blood produced sanguinity, or a brave, hopeful, and amorous disposition; too much phlegm resulted in apathy; black bile led to melancholia; and disproportionate choler caused irascibility and hot-headedness. At the beginning of *Every Man Out of His Humour*, Jonson tells us how humoral theory may be taken as a principle of characterization:

> It may, by Metaphore apply it selfe
> Unto the generall disposition,
> As when some one peculiar qualitie
> Doth so possess a man, that it doth draw
> All his affects, his spirits, and his powers,
> In their confluctions, all to run one way,
> This may be truly said to be a Humor.
>> (Jonson, 1920: Induction, 112–118)

The concept of dominating 'confluctions' is extended even further in Jonson's *Volpone* (1605–06), where greed has caused the characters to become so distorted and dehumanized they take on animal traits, reflected in their names. The old magnifico Volpone is named after a fox, his servant

Mosca, a fly, and the legacy-chasing flatterers Voltore, Corbaccio, and Corvino after carrion-eating vultures, ravens, and crows respectively.

Several aspects of *Volpone*, such as its Venetian setting, reveal the influence of not only the *commedia erudita*, but also the *commedia dell'arte*, an improvised, non-scripted form of 'popular' theatre first recorded in 1545, that based its action around set scenarios that usually involved love intrigues and bits of comic business called *lazzi*. The *commedia dell'arte* employed a stable of reusable characters, most of whom wore expressive stylized masks, each actor dedicating themselves to the study of only one role. The origins of *commedia dell'arte* are obscure, but various types of performance appear to have contributed to its development: the stereotypes of New Comedy, of course, as well as the Roman *fabula* (various types of comic interlude), mime and buffoon shows, mountebanks, carnival processions, and medieval stage devils. The main characters of *commedia* appear to have emerged from four principal types, two infuriating *vecchi*, or old men, usually parents or guardians, and two *zanni*, or clowns, principally responsible for the comedy. These characters came to be fixed into the identifiable roles of Pantalone, the old Venetian merchant; the Doctor, a tiresome pedant; Harlequin, a quasi-independent servant, whose familiar patchwork costume originally signified poverty; and Brighella, a street bully and unrepentant liar who may have helped shape Beaumarchais's Figaro, adopted by Mozart and Rossini. Additional characters developed, each with their own mask, who were to infiltrate and influence Western comic literature in various guises for centuries. These included Pedrolino who was remodelled in France as the sad and lonely Pierrot, and Pulcinella, who eventually became the jovial seaside wife-beater, Mr Punch. In the *commedia*, as well as all the comic forms that utilize stereotypes, identity is destiny, and characters are doomed to repeat their actions and live forever at the mercy of their undiagnosed flaws.

CLOWNS, FOOLS, AND FOLLY

Alongside stereotypes, the predominant figure of comedy is the fool. An historically complex and paradoxical character, claiming a variety of overlapping roles including clown, buffoon, jester, scapegoat, and clairvoyant, the fool recurs as a symbol of contradictions and quandaries. Often the fool is simply a low commoner possessed of shrewd practical sense, as in the popular late medieval tales of the 'obscene and hairy' hunchback Marcolf, who repeatedly proved himself wiser than King Solomon in bouts of wit. Foolishness is not the same as idiocy, but rather an expression of the ambiguous, doubled, and inverted ideas of wisdom and folly that existed in the medieval period. Folly, incorporated into several strong currents of theology, saw foolishness as the overriding characteristic of humanity, revealing itself in all human endeavour. Knowledge was a tainted and problematic concept, as the intolerable desire to know had led to the expulsion from Eden and the fall from grace. God therefore favoured the foolish and inviolable innocents who could not be corrupted by their own ingenuity. Christ had appeared as a manifestation of this humility, presenting himself 'as a mock-king, riding into Jerusalem on an ass, to be displayed in purple, beaten and laughed at . . . Christ and the fool as one in simplicity' (Jacobson, 1997: 167). The ecclesiastical establishment of the Middle Ages incorporated some of these beliefs into their liturgical activities. Church festivals such as the *festum stultorum* (the 'feast of fools'), the *fatuorum papam* (the 'fool's pope'), and the *festum asinorum*, a French feast celebrating Mary's flight into Egypt, during which the priest and congregation were required to bray like donkeys, emphasized the ineffable folly of status in ritual form. As the theologian Peter L. Berger writes, folly enabled a magical transformation of the world, or 'more precisely', was 'an act of magic by which a counterworld [was] made to appear' (Berger, 1997: 193). Yet foolishness for its own sake was neither condoned nor encouraged. Medieval scholasticism made a distinction between the natural and the artificial fool: the first category referred to someone who was considered a 'holy innocent', a child or an adult with a learning disability, whereas the second referred to those 'who counterfeited this state in order to amuse others . . . in short, all clowns' (Palmer, 1994: 43). While clowning was not considered to be a sanctified form of folly, but was equated with vice and sinfulness, the idea of folly as the purifying antidote to human pretension developed as a strong theme in literature. As folly was a conventionalized means of expressing human nature, it could also be adopted as an ironic and paradoxical identity assumed for the purposes of social commentary and satiric attack.

At the close of the Middle Ages, folly became a distinct literary voice, mocking pretension and belittling pride. One of the most significant texts of this kind is Flemish writer Sebastian Brant's *Narrenschiff* (1494), or *Ship of Fools*, a long and popular moral satire that castigated people from all walks of life for their vanity and hypocrisy. Brant's conceit of doomed passengers haplessly sailing to the Land of Fools allowed him to parade a catalogue of social types who failed to meditate on their eternal fate. Brant's text lacks humour, although it was published with a series of lively comic illustrations, but its device of social panorama was employed by a masterpiece of ironic fool literature, Erasmus's *The Praise of Folly* (1511 and 1515). Desiderius Erasmus, the great Dutch humanist and reformer, took the idea for his text from the name of his good friend Sir Thomas More, which, he says, 'is as near to the Greek word for folly, *moria*, as you are from it' (Erasmus, 1993: 4). *The Praise of Folly* is in turns an ironic, ambiguous, and viciously satirical lecture on the benefits of folly delivered by Folly herself. Addressing a happy and receptive crowd who applaud her arrival, Folly, the daughter of Money, nursed by Drunkenness and Ignorance and attended by Self-Love, Flattery, Forgetfulness, Idleness, Pleasure, Madness, and Sensuality, explains her centrality to human affairs. All things are made possible through her mediation, she claims. Peace is the product of flattery, she says, vainglory has resulted in science, wisdom is the fruit of folly as the wise man is modest, but the fool tries, just as Christ used ignorant apostles and told them to think like children. Everywhere, folly is a condition of human nature and without it, social interaction would be unbearable. Consider marriage, for example:

> Goodness me, what divorces or worse than divorces there would be everywhere if the domestic relations of man and wife were not propped up and sustained by the flattery, joking, complaisance, illusions and deceptions provided by my followers! . . . In short, no association or alliance can be happy or stable without me. People can't tolerate a ruler, nor can a master his servant, a maid her mistress . . . unless they sometimes have illusions about each other, make use of flattery, and have the sense to turn a blind eye and sweeten life for themselves with the honey of folly.
>
> (Erasmus, 1993: 35)

Folly, in this case wilful blindness or the willingness to believe convenient fictions, is an essential component of a happy life; humanity is utterly dependent on it. Erasmus intended *The Praise of Folly* as a satire, a comic version of his *On the Education of a Christian Prince* (1516). Through the technique of praising that which is to be condemned, he produced a powerful ironic identity devoted to comic defamiliarization as a means of revealing the truth. Folly, for example, is the only person able to speak freely to monarchs,

> It might be said that the ears of princes shun the truth, and that they steer clear of wise men for the simple reason that they fear there may be someone outspoken enough to risk saying what is true rather than pleasant to hear. The fact is, kings do dislike the truth, but the outcome of this is extraordinary for my fools. They can speak truth and even open insults and be heard with positive pleasure; indeed, the words which would cost a wise man his life are surprisingly enjoyable when uttered by a clown. For truth has a genuine power to please if it manages not to give offence, but this is something the gods have granted only to fools.

> (Erasmus, 1993: 56–57)

The notion of truth emerging in the guise of folly is clearly visible in the work of Shakespeare, where a fool's licence serves a number of dramatic ends. In theatrical practice, the concepts of folly and clowning overlapped considerably. A 'clown' meant literally a person from the country, a yokel whose rusticated ways were cause for mirth. 'Clowning', however, indicated a number of performing skills, such as dancing, juggling, and musicianship. The marriage of clowning skills with folly's penetration of vanity and hierarchy meant that the clowns of the early modern stage became dramatically powerful characters, both agile performers and important narrative units, childishly amusing and insightful by turns.

Shakespeare's use of the clown is established in what is one of his first plays, *The Two Gentlemen of Verona* (1592), where Launce is given a tenuous relationship to the plot that closely follows the action while remaining separate from it. This allows a detached but parallel commentary that unifies themes raised throughout the play's symmetrical pairings of high and low social groups. In the second half of his career, as Shakespeare moved away from writing comedies to concentrate on tragedies and romances, his use of the clown changes in a manner that reflects this new generic context. Around this time (1600), William Kemp, a bumpkin fool who had played most of the early clowns, was replaced in Shakespeare's company by Robert Armin, who seems to have had a much drier and more restrained style. Concomitantly, Shakespeare's later clowns are darker figures, imbued with a sense of mortality and melancholy. The porter of *Macbeth* (1606), for example, imagines himself as the gatekeeper of Hades, while the grave-diggers in *Hamlet* make weary jokes about ageing and physical decomposition, and literally preside over the death of clowning as they dig up the skull of Yorick, Hamlet's favourite jester, now only the memory of laughter. Both *Othello* (1604) and *Antony and Cleopatra* (1606–07) contain only a single clown scene. In the first, the clown jests with Desdemona over the whereabouts of Michael Cassio, a conversation that immediately follows Othello's decision to have Cassio killed. In the second, it is the clown who delivers Cleopatra the venomous asp and wishes her 'joy o'the worm' (Shakespeare, 1989: 5.2.270). Both clowns prefigure deaths, the contrast of the lowly with the elevated lending the *memento mori* a particular piquancy. The most powerful example of this is the fool in *King Lear* (1604–05), who is the only character after Cordelia's banishment able to speak the truth to the king. Lear's fool is rarely funny, but he is frequently barbed and morbidly apposite, openly abusing the old king: 'FOOL. If thou were't my fool, nuncle, I'd have thee beaten for being old before thy time. / LEAR. How's that? / FOOL. Thou shouldst not have been old till thou hadst been / wise' (Shakespeare, 1989: 1.5.36–39). As Lear's rage becomes increasingly impotent and futile, the fool's nonsense is the only appropriate retort. There is no use for him after the third act of the play, but he delivers a prophecy before he goes. Typically paradoxical and impossible, the fool's prophecy imagines the disarray England will fall into when vice is no longer a part of everyday life:

> When slanders do not live in tongues,
> Nor cutpurses come not to throngs,
> When usurers tell their gold i'th'field,
> And bawds and whores do churches build,
> Then shall the realm of Albion
> Come to great confusion;
>
> (Shakespeare, 1989: 3.2.87–92)

The parting speech is indebted to Erasmus's Folly in its belief that self-delusion and hypocrisy are integral to the health of the nation. This central contradiction, the inversion of the good and the bad, the wise and the foolish, and the mad with the sane, lies at the heart of the 'eccentric' vision of comedy, where thoughts and experiences can coexist alongside ironic reflection on those same thoughts.

TRICKSTERS

Paradoxical folly has a close relative in a character known as the 'trickster' who appears in the folk tales and religious myths of many cultures. Mythical tricksters include the Greek god Hermes, a liar, a thief, and a master of disguise; St Peter, who appears in Italian folk tales as a shiftless opportunist whose quasi-criminal activities have to be continually remedied by patient and forgiving Jesus; the Norse god Loki, the companion of the thunder god Thor and personification of lightning; the Native American Coyote, a sacred progenitor, manic omnivore, and externalized taboo; and the Yoruba Esu-Elegabara from Nigeria, a figure who carries the desires of man to the gods, and who limps 'precisely because of his mediating function: his legs are of different lengths because he keeps one anchored in the realm of the gods while the other rests in this, our human world' (Gates Jr, 1988: 6). The trickster is a practical joker, a witty and irreverent being who violates the most sacred of prohibitions. The trickster is not confined by boundaries, conceptual, social, or physical, and can cross lines that are impermeable to normal individuals, between the living and the dead, for example, or to travel between heavenly and human worlds instantaneously. This is why, like Hermes, the trickster often doubles as the messenger of the gods.

The trickster has a religious significance in some cultures that takes a didactic form. Here is an example of a tale featuring 'Coyote', a trickster often found in the Native American cultures of the southwestern United States:

> Hearing a strange sound coming from an old elk skull, Coyote looks inside and finds a village of Ants having a Sun Dance. He makes himself small in order to get inside the skull and see better, but presently his body returns to normal size and his head is stuck inside the skull.

He wanders into a village and announces, 'I am holy; I have super-natural power; you must give me something!' The awe-stricken people pass him in a procession, marking him with pollen as is customary in that region. But the last person in line is a smart aleck boy who is carrying a stick behind his back. When he reaches Coyote he brings the stick down with all of his might across the old elk skull, and it cracks and falls off. 'That's what you should have done long ago', Coyote tells them, 'but instead you wanted too much supernatural power.'

(Hynes and Doty, 1993: 3)

Only after Coyote has been confronted by an equally irreverent adversary does his greed become an admonition of the villagers' gullibility and a warning to treat supernatural events with caution. In this resides Coyote's moral ambiguity: he rightly berates the people, but only after his attempt to cheat them has failed. William Hynes and Thomas Steele see the trickster as a necessary by-product of social order:

Systems normally busy generating firm adherence to their beliefs also maintain within these belief systems, somewhat contradictorily, a raft of tricksters who perpetually invert and profane these same beliefs. In myth and ritual tricksters seem to be officially sanctioned exception clauses by which belief systems regularly satirize themselves.

(Hynes and Steele, 1993: 160)

The trickster, then, provides an integral check on beliefs to prevent them from becoming too secure in themselves.

Trickster figures are everywhere in comedy from disguised lovers to legacy-hunting rakes. Obvious examples would include the cartoon anarchists Bugs Bunny and Daffy Duck, the bogus civil servant Khlestakov in Nikolai Gogol's *The Government Inspector* (1836), or the mute and infuriating Harpo Marx. In Roman New Comedy, trickster figures inhabit the skin of the ingenious slave character. In Plautus' *Pseudolus* (c.191 BC), the slave Pseudolus, his name itself meaning 'false one', addresses the audience with a proclamation:

Now let all take notice – and let none say he has not received notice – all adults here present, all citizens of this city, all friends and

acquaintances of mine, are hereby warned and advised, this day . . . to
be on their guard . . . gainst me . . . and not to trust a word I say.

(Plautus, 1984: 221)

Pseudolus' low social status gives him the freedom to move across social
boundaries, which includes awareness of the fictive nature of his existence,
operating both within the frame of the fiction and without it, addressing
the audience and acknowledging the fact of the performance, and at one
stage even admitting to being an actor. Within the play, his trickster
mobility makes him an intermediary between the lover, the patrician
parent, the pimp and prostitute, between illicit and legitimate love and
respectable and shameful liaisons. In the end, Pseudolus forges domestic
harmony from sexual and financial scandal and consolidates the system
by flouting it.

Shakespeare's Puck is similarly the counter-intuitive provider of
solutions in *A Midsummer Night's Dream*. Puck, also known as Robin
Goodfellow, is a genius of minor mischief and domestic upsets, a 'merry
wanderer of the night' devoted to practical jokes and turning sentiment
into laughter:

The wisest aunt, telling the saddest tale,
Sometime for three-foot stool mistaketh me;
Then I slip from her bum, down topples she,
And 'tailor' cries, and falls into a cough,
And then the whole quire hold their hips and loffe,
And waxen in their mirth, and neeze, and swear
A merrier hour was never wasted there.

(Shakespeare, 1989: 2.1.50–57)

Puck is in fact a collation of a number of spirits, including hobgob-
lins, changelings, and incubi. In the generations immediately prior to
Shakespeare, fairies like Puck were styled as sinister demons who 'stole
children, dispensed sudden illnesses, destroyed crops and flocks and were
believed to live in hell' (Laroque, 1993: 22). The transformation of Puck
from demonic spirit to playful trickster is partly due to the falling away of
superstitious belief, as well as the transposition of character types from

classical literature onto domestic writing. As Jonathan Gil Harris writes, the supernatural characters of *A Midsummer Night's Dream* are a

> syncretic blend of powerful yet for the most part benevolent spirits taken from the seemingly disparate domains of Greek mythology, courtly romance and village folklore; even . . . Puck is a composite of 'high' and 'low', owing as much to Neoplatonic conceptions of Cupid as to the Robin Goodfellow of popular tradition.

(Harris, 1998: 353–354)

In the psychoanalytic system of Carl Jung, the trickster is a remnant of an earlier state of consciousness before humanity had become fully civilized. In Jung's view 'all mythical figures correspond to inner psychic experiences and originally sprang from them' (Jung, 1959, vol. 9: 256). Jung sees the cycles of tales that feature the trickster as a means of narrating how 'a higher level of consciousness has covered up a lower one' (Jung, 1959, vol. 9: 266). Trickster narratives usually conclude with the meddlesome actions of the protagonist coming to serve some useful or illustrative purpose, as in the case of Coyote. As such, argues Jung, they mirror the development of human consciousness from a wilder and more savage state to a state of relative sophistication. 'The civilizing process begins with the framework of the trickster cycle itself', he writes. 'The marks of deepest unconsciousness fall away from him; instead of acting in a brutal, savage, stupid, and senseless fashion, the trickster's behaviour towards the end of the cycle becomes quite useful and sensible' (Jung, 1959, vol. 9: 266). Such is the trajectory of Puck, who initially serves as an agent of chaos, but is ultimately responsible for inducing Demetrius to love Helena and arranging the young couples in perfect symmetry, so that 'Jack shall have Jill / Nought shall go ill; / The man shall have his mare again, and all shall be well' (Shakespeare, 1989: 3.2.461–3).

While Jung thought of the trickster as the 'shadow' of a former being, whose high visibility in narrative speaks of its refusal to be completely dissolved into modern consciousness, structural anthropologist Claude Lévi-Strauss saw him as a symbolic agent who unified two otherwise contradictory concepts in the structure of understanding. In 'The Structural Study of Myth' (1958), Lévi-Strauss argues that in traditional cultures, two opposite and irreconcilable terms, such as life and death, are replaced by equivalent terms, such as agriculture and hunting, in order that a third term might be permitted as an intermediary. This is why carrion-eating animals like the coyote and the raven are given the role of tricksters in Native American myths. These animals possess some of the elements of both terms: they are like hunters because they eat meat, but also like farmers because they do not kill what they eat. 'The trickster', he says, 'is a mediator. Since his mediating function occupies a position halfway between two polar terms, he must retain something of that duality – namely an ambiguous and equivocal character' (Lévi-Strauss, 1963: 226). The comic mobility of the trickster, therefore, is a means of bringing about reconciliation through the interpenetration of apparently irreconcilable realms of existence. By having a foot in both the sub- and super-lunary worlds and embodying a moral ambiguity, he acts as a signifier in which opposites can come together: through the mediation of the trickster, life and death are reconciled.

WIT, CAMP, AND BATHOS: CONGREVE, WILDE, HANCOCK

The versions of subjectivity we have seen so far have all been grounded in some sense of the truth of identity: whether it be the sanctified ambiguity of fool or trickster, or the supposed universality of types. In this final section, we shall look at comic techniques that arose in the late seventeenth century that demonstrate a different attitude towards identity, which we might think of as characteristically ironic, dramatically individualistic, and largely agnostic. These techniques would be 'wit', celebrated in Restoration and eighteenth-century literary culture; 'camp', the knowing elevation of style and debonair dismissal of gravity; and 'bathos', the puncturing intrusion of reality that floors lofty aspirations. All three techniques are generally associated with urban and sophisticated comedies from the seventeenth century onwards, comedies permeated with a non-committal individualism and defiance towards seriousness and orthodoxy. In Restoration comedy, the quality of wit, quick inventiveness in language, and taking pleasurable liberties with meanings, is a fashionable way of asserting social superiority and individuality above the ordinary dullness of society. This idea is derived in part from earlier conduct books, such as Baldesar Castiglione's *The Book of the Courtier* (1528) that declares witticisms 'diverting and sophisticated', and considers spontaneous displays of wit perfect examples of the courtly ideal of *sprezzatura*, or effortless grace and accomplishment (Castiglione, 1986: 172). The plots of Restoration comedy differ from their renaissance predecessors inasmuch as the desires of the individual take priority over the needs of the community, as, writes Edward Burns, '"Wit" – the ability to use social and linguistic artifice for personal ends – overrides "decorum" – the affirmation of an intrinsically self-righting social order – and thus plays reach their endings on kinds of contracts, not an order re-discovered, presumed to have been somehow always "there" and hence presented as natural' (Burns, 1987: 17). This change reveals a new disillusionment with ideologies of absolute order following the social upheavals of the English Civil War. Authority had disgraced itself, it seemed, and sincerity and conviction were currencies debased by ideology. For Joseph Addison, writing in 1711, people were no longer marked by 'a noble Simplicity of Behaviour', but had become expert 'in Doggerel, Humour, Burlesque, and all the trivial Arts of Ridicule' (Addison and Steele, 1979, vol. 2: 238). With this post-lapsarian cynicism came the enormous popularity of parody and irony as literary modes. This would also account for the centrality of artifice and 'playing' as themes in the comedy of this era, confirmed by its extravagant use of masks, disguises, impersonations, and subterfuges that focus attention on the theme of credibility. Richard Brinsley Sheridan's *The Critic* (1779) represents the culmination of knowing meta-theatricality of this kind, as the entire piece, set at a rehearsal, is an extended parody of literary and dramatic conventions continually interrupted by inept discussions of style and merit. William Congreve's *The Way of the World* (1700) opens just after its hero Mirabell has lost a card game, and it continues to dramatize the theme of playing for high stakes until it ends. In this play, performance, the appearance of action, and the concealment of intention, is unproblematically offered as the route to gratification and reward. The Restoration comic hero is a male fantasy of libertinage, where wit is a verbal manifestation of virility that presides over the fops and the Witwouds, gaining wealth, respect, and women as returns.

The arch-sophistication of Algernon Moncrieff, the louche aristocrat of Oscar Wilde's *The Importance of Being Earnest* (1895), presents a further development of the witty, noncommittal, and 'performed' comic persona. Algy, utterly self-absorbed, exists in a perpetually ironized relationship to the society in which he lives, in which contradictions are the foundation for knowledge: 'More than half of modern culture depends on what one shouldn't read', he says (Wilde, 1980: 1.131–132). His friend Jack Worthing enjoys land, income, and position as a Justice of the Peace, but lacks a family history and therefore 'an assured basis for a recognized position in good society' (Wilde, 1980: 1.579–580). At the heart of the play is the plasticity of identity: Jack is 'Ernest in town and Jack in the country' (Wilde, 1980: 1.168), while Algy is an enthusiastic 'Bunburyist', an author of fictional persons, who becomes Ernest in the country. In the twice-invented Ernest we have the perfect emblem of identity in Wilde's world, all surface and no content. Embodied twice in Jack and Algy, Ernest is simultaneously two people and no one at all. *The Importance of Being Earnest* is therefore a play about the multiplication of a central identity that is notable because of its absence. At face value, its anxieties concern the expectations of high society and the importance of conforming to them. From the manner in which the criteria are filled, however, changing names, adopting false identities, the fortunate coincidence of Miss Prism's retrospectively legitimizing narrative, reminiscent of the recognition scene of New Comedy, it is clear that authenticity is secondary to the maintenance of appearances and contorting oneself to fit the bill. While the title insists on the importance of honesty, the play itself resounds with inconsistent and contradictory pronouncements for the purposes of stylish effect. Gwendolen and Cecily's resolve to be scandalized, for example, is a performance of being scandalized, rather than the thing itself:

> GWENDOLEN. Let us preserve a dignified silence.
>
> CECILY. Certainly. It's the only thing to do now.
>
> *Enter* JACK *followed by* ALGERNON. *They whistle some dreadful popular air from a British Opera.*
>
> GWENDOLEN. This dignified silence seems to produce an unpleasant effect.
>
> CECILY. A most distasteful one.
>
> GWENDOLEN. But we will not be the first to speak.
>
> CECILY. Certainly not.
>
> GWENDOLEN. Mr Worthing, I have something very particular to ask you . . .
>
> (Wilde, 1980: 3.12–17)

The Importance of Being Earnest fits exactly the criteria for what the influential American cultural critic Susan Sontag has described as 'Camp'. 'Camp', she says, 'is a certain mode of aestheticism. It is one way of seeing the world as an aesthetic phenomenon . . . not in terms of beauty but in terms of the degree of artifice, of stylization' (Sontag, 1982: 106). Published in 1964, 'Notes on Camp' anticipates some postmodernist discussion of the triumph of style, but actually finds its origins in much older forms such as Mannerism and eighteenth-century literary excess. 'Camp sees everything in quotation marks', she writes, it is to 'understand Being-as-Playing-a-Role' (Sontag, 1982: 109). As Gwendolyn says, 'in matters of grave importance, style, not sincerity, is the vital thing' (Wilde, 1980: 2.28–29). Wilde's own aesthetic beliefs held that art was essentially useless, but that its lack of utility was the source of its beauty. That art existed only for its own sake made it independent of the world and therefore liberated from it, a liberation that left art free to concentrate on its beauty, and 'the sheer absoluteness of its detachment' (Leggatt, 1998: 34).

In the twentieth century, Wilde's sophisticated style continued in the work of Noël Coward. Coward, 'a man who spent a life-time merchandising his deluxe persona' (Lahr, 1984: 22) was a prolific writer of prose, drama, and over three hundred published songs, all of which were characterized by effortless wit and laissez-faire charm. Like Wilde's aristocrats, Coward's characters enjoy their own fictionality. The divorced and reunited couple of *Private Lives* (1930), for example, share flippancy as a philosophy of life, and a defence against reality:

> AMANDA. Don't laugh at me, I'm serious.
>
> ELYOT [*seriously*]. You musn't be serious, my dear one; it's just what they want.
>
> AMANDA. Who's they?
>
> ELYOT. All the futile moralists who try to make life unbearable. Laugh at them. Be flippant. Laugh at everything, all their sacred shibboleths. Flippancy brings out the acid in their damned sweetness and light.
>
> AMANDA. If I laugh at everything, I must laugh at us too.
>
> ELYOT. Certainly you must. We're figures of fun all right.
>
> (Coward, 1999: 226–227)

In Wilde and Coward, then, comic identity is conceived as a means of refusing incorporation into a communal identity defined by the sobriety of the establishment. In both cases there is a celebration of individualism over the masses, an elitist appreciation of privilege over all that is dull and ordinary, and a belief that easy intelligence equals freedom from conformity.

The underside of Wilde and Coward, and the immersion in ordinariness is what characterizes the bathetic hero. Bathos, the reduction of the elevated to the everyday to produce an incongruous anticlimax, is a rhetorical term whose current usage is taken from Alexander Pope's Scriblerian tract *Peri Bathous, or the Art of Sinking in Poetry* (1727). Bathetic comedy, moments where romantic or glamorous concepts are found to be untenable when pushed up against reality, became particularly popular after World War II, and may express the antipathy towards Cowardesque privilege felt by the newly enfranchised working men and women of the nationalized industries. The bathetic hero is perhaps the comic equivalent of the 'angry young man' of the 1950s, continually reminded of the imperatives of conformity, and the poverty of ambition amongst the working class. The bathetic hero is poised to reflect on the distance between ideological fictions and reality like the marginalized voice of folly in the consumer age. Dark versions of comic bathos appear in the work of Joe Orton and Harold Pinter, both of whom use laughter as a means of attacking middle-class sensibility and hypocritical establishment values, but the model for the bathetic hero in British comedy is Tony Hancock (1924–68), whose popular radio show *Hancock's Half Hour* transferred to television in 1956 and ran for five years. Everything was slightly disappointing in Hancock's world, and cause for heightened incredulity. Stephen Wagg calls his persona 'the model of a dyspeptic, status-anxious, petit-bourgeois suburbanite stomping grumpily about the lower reaches of Middle England' (Wagg, 1998: 7). Hancock was an unemployed actor with delusions of grandeur, living in rented accommodation in Railway Cuttings in East Cheam, his address an emblem of dishevelment, with his resolutely working-class housemate, played by Sid James. An episode called *The Big Night* (1959) that sees Hancock and Sid preparing for a blind date, might be thought of as a lower middle-class revision of the aristocratic comedies of sophistication. Mimicking Coward, Hancock imagines himself an international playboy, yet as a subject of the working week his play is confined to Saturday night only and his leisure strictly dictated by time. This is the consistent theme of the *Hancock* series, the distance that emerges between the concept of the self generated by the individual desiring ego, especially one who 'was not only forever seeking to better himself but believed at the same time that he was already superior', and that produced by the reality of economic status (Neal and Krutnik, 1990: 248). Not only is Hancock economically confined, but we find there are erotic limits imposed on him as well. Sid's hyperbolized physical description of Hancock's blind date, built up by swelling romantic music, abruptly ends when we learn that her name is Gladys. Similarly, Hancock's home, the place where he should be master, revolts against him in the form of his elderly maid, Mrs Cravat. Mrs Cravat refuses to conform to any of the conventions of polite domestic service, just as Hancock fails to be an aristocrat: she is surly, aggressive, rude, and dismissive of Hancock's pretensions to social nicety, even amplifying his own pomposity by bringing in the breakfast and announcing it as '*oeuf scambléd*', scrambled eggs, transformed through bad French into a parody of an expensive restaurant. The expanse between Hancock's bathetic mediocrity and the glamour to which he continually aspired was also the subject of a film-length treatment, *The Rebel* (1960), in which he travels to Paris to become an artist, enjoying immense success despite an acute lack of ability. By the end of this film we are thoroughly convinced that high art is fraudulent nonsense, and the best thing that Hancock can do is return to the suburbs and remain an eccentric. In this sense, bathos is not only a voicing of one's imprisonment within class structures, but also a statement of reconciliation that acknowledges suburban 'normality' as the only identity that is truly honest and decent.

In summary, we might say that comic identity appears to be found in a sense of division or incompleteness. This can manifest itself as a conflict between alternative world views, between appearance and reality or between self-image and public perception. It might also be the case that a character is not fully attuned to the world nor entirely possessed of a sense of themselves or their surroundings. Obliviousness to the demands of everyday life might be invigorating, but it also condemns characters to repeat the pattern of their mistakes. In an historical context, to such dividedness there is attributed a philosophical or mythic dimension, as in the case of folly and tricksterism, that asserts the existence of a universe outside the individual and a higher power that controls it. In the modern age, the dividedness of comic identity and the fluidity of meanings that accompany it could be read as symbols of increasingly individualistic egos and the estrangement of self and society. Either way, comic humans are incomplete.

3

GENDER AND SEXUALITY

I don't like funny women. I come out of a generation where the woman should be beautiful and sexy and a wonderful flower attached to a man, even though my whole life has been the antithesis of this. To this day, you don't expect women to be funny.

Joan Rivers

Comedy treats matters of sex more often and more openly than any other form. Its festive structure and Dionysial associations afford sexual themes greater freedom, while also providing a fictional arena in which taboos may be openly discussed without fear of social contamination. The unquestioned bed-sharing and co-dependency of partners like Laurel and Hardy and Morecambe and Wise is evidence of a loosening of the usual rules, just as the enormous popularity of a number of openly gay comedians, such as Julian Clary or Graham Norton, both of whom have made effeminacy and homosexual innuendo central to their act, seems to be at odds with a society that remains largely homophobic. Of course, comedy places sexual desire and erotic arousal within the context of laughter, rendering discussions furtive, titular, and self-conscious, and complicating its aims. Freud writes that 'the spheres of sexuality and obscenity offer the amplest occasions for obtaining comic pleasure . . . for they can show human beings in their dependence on bodily needs . . . or they can reveal the physical demands lying behind the claim of mental love' (Freud, 2001: 222). In both cases, sexual themes amuse because some masked or elided aspect of the animal subject peeps through the civilized exterior and shows itself to be insatiable. Studies of sexual content in humour, such as G. Legman's two-volume *Rationale of the Dirty Joke* (1975) or Christopher Wilson's scientific study of joke function, stress that sexual jokes 'offer the furtive joy of ignoring taboos' (Wilson, 1979: 131). Yet while sexual content in comedy may be pleasurable because it outruns censorship, it is also important to acknowledge the extent to which sexual themes play a part in establishing or consolidating norms of sexual behaviour. Wilson discusses the use and effect of incest jokes, for example, and concludes that 'Humour that dismisses incest and other socially disapproved relationships as "laughable" may be seen to illustrate and reinforce sexual convention' (Wilson, 1979: 177). Similarly, as US comedian Joan Rivers testifies, we may view comedy's representation of male and female gender roles, especially in narratives that conclude in marriage, as confirmations of culturally orthodox views of the nature of men and women. Jimmy Durante's crack, 'my wife has a slight impediment in her speech. Every now and then she stops to breathe', or Groucho Marx's 'women should be obscene and not heard', are both mid-twentieth-century verifications of the patriarchal view of women as incessantly verbose in violation of their ideal role as sexually attractive objects. Comedy therefore articulates sexual politics from a number of contradictory positions, including liberation from censorship, exploration of desire, and insistence on conservative categories of gender.

CROSS-DRESSING: *AS YOU LIKE IT* AND *SOME LIKE IT HOT*

A familiar motif in the comic exploration of sexuality is the cross-dressing 'progress narrative'. According to Majorie Garber, a transvestite progress narrative is a plot that requires one or more of its characters to disguise their gender 'in order to get a job, escape repression, or gain artistic or political "freedom"' (Garber, 1992: 70). There are many examples of this in comedy, including the plays *Charley's Aunt* (1892) and *La Cage Aux Folles* (1978), the movies *Mrs Doubtfire* (1993), *Tootsie, Victor/Victoria* (both 1982), and *Some Like It Hot* (1959), and the cross-dressing comedies of Shakespeare, *As You Like It*, *Twelfth Night*, and *The Merchant of Venice*.

In *As You Like It*, cross-dressing allows the play to develop a heightened eroticism and an inclusive attitude towards sexuality, and even the title suggests a relaxed attitude to sex – the 'it' presumably a reference to all kinds of appetites, not only sexual. 'It' is a good word to use in relation to the sexual tensions of this play, as they are at once indeterminate, elliptical, and absolutely central to the plot. *As You Like It* is the story of Rosalind and her companion Celia, forced by the usurper Duke Frederick to follow her father into exile in the Forest of Arden. Aware of the danger facing lone women travellers as 'Beauty provoketh thieves sooner than gold' (Shakespeare, 1989: 1.3.109), Rosalind decides to disguise herself as a man:

> Because that I am more than common tall,
> That I did suit me all points like a man,
> A gallant curtal-axe upon my thigh,
> A boar-spear in my hand, and in my heart,
> Lie there what hidden woman's fear there will.
> (Shakespeare, 1989: 1.3.114–118)

Taking up the props of masculinity, and burying 'female' traits such as apprehension, Rosalind completes her transformation and takes the name 'Ganymede'. The Shakespearean stage used boy actors in female roles exclusively, as women were forbidden from performing in public and did not take parts in plays until the Restoration. That all of Shakespeare's female roles, even the most demanding tragic ones, were played by boys without reducing drama to farce, tells us that this convention makes Rosalind's gender swap utterly convincing within the context of the play. But *As You Like It* is complicated by an additional layer of transformation. Rosalind's male disguise reminds us of the initial gender of the performer, highlighting the fact that his femaleness is only theatrical, with the effect of blurring gender distinctions while accentuating them thematically. This gender ambiguity appears to be at the centre of sexual fascination in the play, and instead of protecting her from unwanted attention, Rosalind's disguise makes the apparent youthful maleness of her character its central sexual object. The cross-dressing of *As You Like It* therefore encourages the boy actor to assume a heightened erotic presence by placing him in the playful and indeterminate world of comic identities. The key to this is the choice of the name 'Ganymede' with which Rosalind completes her disguise. In Greek mythology, Ganymede was a beautiful Trojan youth, so admired by Zeus he was taken as his lover. There is a deliberateness in Rosalind naming herself after 'Jove's own page' (Shakespeare, 1989: 1.3.124); the choice introduces the idea of men as compelling sexual objects, usurping women in the traditional role of the desired one (underlined perhaps by the un-cross-dressed Celia's choice of name, 'Aliena', pushing women further to the margins). The naming of Ganymede ensures that Rosalind will be at the heart of a series of crossed and interacting desiring relationships that centre specifically on the strange and alluring identity she has created for herself. Chief amongst these are two fascinations that would now be labelled as homosexual. First, the desire of Phoebe for Rosalind, which displaces the shepherd Silvius, her appropriate and conventional mate; and second, more important, the apparent fascination that Orlando has for Ganymede irrespective of his proclaimed love for Rosalind. Ganymede's interactions with those he fascinates are characterized by verbal sparring and witty comebacks. Stephen Greenblatt sees this as a stage version of sexual excitement. 'Dallying with words is the principal Shakespearian representation of erotic heat', he writes. 'Hence his plots go out of their way to create not only obstacles in the lovers' path but occasions for friction between them' (Greenblatt, 1988: 90). The contest of Beatrice and Benedict in *Much Ado About Nothing* (1598) exemplifies this kind of verbal foreplay, but in the green world of Arden, the friction caused between man and boy appears to condone alternative desiring partnerships outside the compulsory heterosexuality of the town. Given these circumstances, Stephen Orgel sees a radical sexual agenda at work in the play, calling Ganymede a 'dangerous alternative' to heterosexual norms and reproductive sexuality, as 'the idea of the boy displacing the woman appears in its most potentially threatening form, the catamite for whom Jove abandons his marriage bed' (Orgel, 1997: 57). Evidence for this can be found in the 'wooing scenes' of acts 3 and 4, in which Ganymede proposes to take Rosalind's place and invites Orlando to practise his seduction of Rosalind upon him: 'woo me, woo me, for now I am in a / holiday humour, and like enough to consent', she/he says (Shakespeare, 1989: 4.1.64–65). Orlando, wholeheartedly embracing the fantasy Ganymede has proposed, pleads with him:

> ORL. Then love me, Rosalind.
> ROS. Yes, faith, will I, Fridays and Saturdays and all.
> ORL. And wilt thou have me?
> ROS. Ay, and twenty such.
> ORL. What sayst thou?
> ROS. Are you not good?
> ORL. I hope so.
> ROS. Why then, can one desire too much of a good thing? (*to Celia*)
>   Come, sister, you shall be the priest and marry us – Give me your
>   hand Orlando. – What do you say sister?
> ORL. (*to Celia*) Pray thee, marry us.
>
>   (Shakespeare, 1989: 4.1.107–119)

So happy is Orlando to accept Ganymede as Rosalind that he pleads with Celia to marry them and allow the boy to displace the woman in the marriage rite. That this was not entirely acceptable in its day is evinced by the early modern opponents of the stage who condemned the erotic lure of theatre practice and considered the presence of the boy player to encourage homosexuality. John Rainolds, in *Th'overthrow of Stage-Plays* (1599), warned that the kisses of boy actors could so turn a man that he could be moved to infidelity: 'If they do but touch men only with their mouth, they put them to wonderful pain and make them mad, so beautiful boys by kissing does sting and pour secretly in a kind of poison' (quoted in Orgel, 1997: 28). Philip Stubbes's *Anatomy of Abuses* (1583) held that public performances, with their 'wanton gestures' and 'bawdy speeches', were a place for men to meet for the purpose of finding a sexual partner. After the play was done, 'everyone brings another homeward of their very friendly, and in their secret conclaves, covertly, they play the sodomites, or worse' (quoted in Orgel, 1997: 29). For Orgel, these anti-theatrical attacks offer three very important insights into the connection between sexuality and the early modern stage. Although he emphasizes the ideological extremity of opponents to theatre, he concludes that their arguments indicate, first, that 'the basic form of response to theatre is erotic; second, that erotically, theatre is uncontrollably exciting; and third, that the basic, essential form of erotic excitement in men is homosexual – that, indeed, women are only a cover for men' (Orgel, 1989: 17).

Billy Wilder's 1959 film, voted the best comedy of all time by the American Film Institute, brings the cross-dressing theme into the twentieth century. *Some Like It Hot* shares many similarities with *As You Like It*, not least the indeterminate and enticing 'it' of the title. The film restates the idea that men can adequately replace women, both as women and as sexual partners for men, and that femininity does not reside in biological gender or ontological identity, but in 'feminine', material supplements to the body such as high heels, make-up, and brassieres. The film tells the story of two Depression-era musicians, Joe and Jerry, played by Tony Curtis and Jack Lemmon, who witness a mob killing and are forced to go into hiding. They dress as women, rename themselves Josephine and Daphne, and join 'Sweet Sue's Society Syncopators', an all-girl jazz band travelling on an engagement to Florida. Joe falls in love with the band's singer, Sugar, played by Marilyn Monroe, which necessitates the adoption of a further identity as 'Shell Jr', in a ploy conceived in answer to Sugar's fantasy of a rich man in glasses. Joe and Jerry, motivated by the threat of death, come to understand quickly that the authenticity of 'femaleness' resides only in the quality of its performance. For example, when joining the band for the first time, they struggle with their disguises until they find an example to emulate in Marilyn Monroe:

> JER. (*rubbing his ankle*) How can they walk on these things? How do they keep their balance?
>
> JOE. Must be the way their weight is distributed. Come on.

> *As they proceed along the platform, a gust of wind sends their skirts billowing. Jerry stops again and pulls his skirt down.*

> JER. And it's so drafty. They must be catching colds all the time.
>
> JOE. (*urging him on*) Quit stalling. We'll miss the train.
>
> JER. I feel so naked. Like everybody's looking at me.
>
> JOE. With those legs? Are you crazy?
>
> JER. (*stopping in his tracks*) It's no use. We'll never get away with it, Joe.
>
> JOE. The name is Josephine. And it was your idea in the first place.

> . . . *a member of the girls' band comes hurrying past them, carrying a valise and ukulele case. Her name is SUGAR . . .*
>
> JER.   Who are we kidding? Look at that – look how she moves – it's like jello on springs – they must have some sort of a built-in motor. I tell you it's a whole different sex.
>
> (Wilder, 1959)

Simply wearing women's clothes seems to accentuate the men's sense of essential sexual differences, as well as underline their view of women as sex objects. But once given insight into the tricks of the performance, 'jello on springs' accompanied by a close-up of Monroe's backside in motion, they copy it and are successfully assimilated into the band with absolutely no suspicions raised. The transvestism of the two leading men is, of course, foisted upon them, and we are continually reminded that their cross-dressing is a means to an end, not evidence of a latent fetish. To remind us, Joe and Jerry's clothing is continually depicted as costume, complicated and unusual and always requiring adjustment and therefore risible in its unnaturalness when contrasted with their fundamental maleness. However, while a masculine authenticity is alluded to beneath the clothes, women themselves remain conspicuously facile. Monroe's Sugar is portrayed as a stereotype of a certain kind of woman. Singing 'I Wanna Be Loved By You', Monroe wears a tight dress that accentuates her bosom by appearing to be translucent. Amidst the 'conscious heightening as well as dissolving of sexual stereotypes' that Bruce Babington and Peter William Evans see at work in this film, Monroe represents 'overflowing female excess' (Babington and Evans, 1989: 227–228), a figure of hyperbolic femininity that Molly Haskell describes as being 'as much in "drag"' as Joe and Jerry (quoted in Sikov, 1994: 142). During the song, which tells of passive availability and urges the lover to approach, so much is made of Monroe's bosom that rather than guaranteeing hers as an authentic female body amongst the fakes, she appears as an unrealistic construct and a product of 'glamour', Hollywood, and girlie magazines. As Ed Sikov writes, 'If the film has a central deficiency, it is Wilder's inability to move Monroe's character beyond a sort of paralysed observation of her own image' (Sikov, 1994: 143). Even 'real' women seem to lack substance beyond the trappings of their gender.

Structurally, *Some Like It Hot* and *As You Like It* are close. Both feature the removal from the hostile and dangerous city: in Shakespeare's play it is the court under the tyrannical Duke Frederick, in Wilder's film a violent Chicago of gangsters, prohibition, unemployment, and hunger. Both the Forest of Arden and Miami Beach represent liberation from danger and the opportunity to explore alternative identities and the fermentation of romantic relationships. Both locations are associated with holidays and respite from economic demands, as Rosalind says to Orlando, 'There's / no clock in the forest' (Shakespeare, 1989: 3.2.294–295). It seems both film and play insist that the fluctuation of playful identities is only a temporary measure, necessary to reconfirm heterosexual norms which Majorie Garber sees as fundamentally unchanged by the period of cross-dressing:

> The ideological patterns of this implication are clear: cross-dressing can be 'fun' or 'functional' so long as it occupies a liminal space and a temporary time period; after this carnivalization, however . . . the cross-dresser is expected to resume life as he or she was, having, presumably, recognized the touch of 'femininity' or 'masculinity' in her or his otherwise 'male' or 'female' self.
>
> (Garber, 1992: 70)

When we look at the endings of both narratives, however, we can see that they refuse to relinquish their hold on the carnival world absolutely, and that more than a 'touch' of the freer desiring relationships and gender identifications they have discovered remains after the narrative ends. In the epilogue to *As You Like It*, the actor playing Rosalind comes out of character, addressing the audience with conventional pleas for leniency before saying to the men:

> If I were a woman I would kiss as many of you as had
> beards that pleased me, complexions that liked me, and
> breaths that I defied not. And I am sure as many as
> have good beards, or good faces, or sweet breaths will
> for my kind offer, when I make curtsy, bid me farewell.
>
> (Shakespeare, 1989: Epilogue, 16–21)

At the end of *Some Like It Hot*, Jerry, still disguised as Daphne, offers a series of reasons why he cannot marry Osgood Fielding III, the millionaire who has fervently pursued him, finally admitting 'Damn it, I'm a man'. Osgood's reply is the pragmatic 'Nobody's perfect'. Such a wonderfully reasonable response intimates that heterosexuality is not necessary for a perfectly good marriage. Rosalind, revealed finally as a boy actor offering to kiss the men, suggests that the sexuality of *As You Like It* is not contained entirely by the parameters of the fiction, but is 'diffuse, non-localized, and inclusive, extending to the audience an invitation to "come play"' (Traub, 1992: 142). Both endings suggest the possibility of the homoeroticism of the cross-dressed period continuing in the world after the issues that forced characters into disguise have been resolved. Indeed, Ed Sikov emphatically says of Jerry's situation, 'Osgood's final declaration is openly gay, there's no question about that. The line is meaning-less otherwise' (Sikov, 1994: 146). Sikov, chiding critics who claim that '"Nobody's perfect" is not specifically about gay sexuality', points out their wish to 'steal what precious little mainstream cultural participation gay men and lesbians can claim for ourselves. Somehow it doesn't seem fair' (Sikov, 1994: 148).

DRAG AND TRANSVESTISM

The reluctantly cross-dressed protagonist of a progress narrative is a substantially different prospect from the female impersonator, or drag act, that has been a successful comic franchise since the mid-1800s. Here, drag is not donned as a means to achieve an end in the conventionally dressed world, but is the focus of the entire performance. The female impersonator derived in part from nineteenth-century circus acts that tricked their audiences into believing that daring acrobats and gymnasts were in fact dainty girls to enhance their box-office appeal, as well as the tradition of men playing women's roles in minstrel shows. 'Putting on the drag' originally meant applying the brakes of a carriage, but once the word had entered homosexual slang through the 'molly-houses' or transvestite clubs of nineteenth-century London, it stood to mean the 'drag of a gown with a train' (Senelick, 2000: 302). Early drag acts conventionally con-cluded with the removal of the wig to reveal the close-cropped hair that acted as a guarantor of the performer's masculinity, a gesture that places great signifying emphasis on the coiffure, as in the finale of Ben Jonson's *Epicoene* (1609–10). In music hall, the term 'female impersonator' was commonly used to describe drag acts, a label that makes the performer's gender self-evident. For comic drag, whose best-known mainstream exponents are performers like Danny La Rue, Barry Humphries as Dame Edna Everage, and Paul O'Grady as Lily Savage, the intention is to parody types of femininity through a knowing masculine prism that acknowledges the nature of the travesty at all times. The question of what is being parodied is largely dependent on the performer, but generally drag allows the male comedian to exploit his attire to offer a deliberately provoking perspective on women. This amounts to a form of ventriloquism that explores women's attitudes to sex, women's conversation, and monologues intended to puncture idealized versions of femininity. In the tradition of pantomime dames, comic drag paints a picture of feminine grotesque, self-delusion, hyperbolized glamour and sexual outrageousness that would be inappropriate in 'real' women (although this is also true of Caroline Aherne's 'Mrs Merton' character). Danny La Rue, who was enormously successful in Britain in the 1970s, with his own nightclub, television series, and appearance at Royal Variety shows, assumed the persona of a raucous showgirl with lower middle-class manners and a crass addiction to extraordinary outfits, high wigs, and sparkling accessories. La Rue's prime-time popularity and insistence on being a 'family act' meant that much of the sexual tension in drag was removed from his show. La Rue was keen to point out that what he parodied was artifice in women, especially a certain kind of woman he found vulgar. Laurence Senelick sees this as a contradiction, writing that La Rue creates an 'anodyne illusion' that mocks overly sexualized women, while simultaneously placing them at the centre of a family show (Senelick, 2000: 247). Lily Savage, his postmodern alternative, to whom glamour is distinctly foreign, is a 6' 2" peroxide blond from Birkenhead, first unveiled in the gay cabaret of London's Vauxhall Tavern in 1985. Wearily smoking onstage, she is resigned to petty brutality and failure while acknowledging the free-market nature of sexuality in the underground economy. In both the financial success that putting on drag has brought Paul O'Grady as well as Lily's own history of low-grade prostitution, the selling of women is always thematically near.

How might we then think about the representation of gender through drag acts and female impersonators? Certainly the politics of drag have produced a number of theoretical perspectives on its representation of gender, although it must be acknowledged that these are almost exclusively concerned with the meaning of drag in gay and lesbian culture, where comedy is not always the primary focus of the act. Esther Newton, writing in 1979, argued that drag existed within a two-tier 'sartorial system' in which the gender identification of the performer was best understood in relation to the first two layers of their clothing. The top layer of clothing, visible on the outside, was a 'costume' and presumed to be part of an act or symbolic presentation on behalf of the wearer. The second layer of clothing, essentially underwear, hidden from view, reveals the true nature of the wearer's gender identification that 'anchors' their gender during the performance. Thus, Newton argues, drag, 'poses an opposition between one sex-role sartorial system and the "self", whose identity has to be indicated in some way', because, 'when impersonators are performing, the oppositional play is between "appearance" which is female, and "reality", or "essence", which is male' (Newton, 1979: 101). Drag is then a parodic interplay between 'appearance' and 'essence', in which the performer retains their 'real' gender via the guarantee of the concealed body. Applying Newton's position to comic drag, we might conclude that its garish make-up, euphemistic sexual content, and parody of female behaviour amounts to mimicry and mockery of women by men who always confidently remain men. Yet Newton's sartorial distinction remains questionable: how can one set of clothes be said to stand for gender authenticity, while another represents quotation and parody? Mark Simpson, for example, has argued that drag can go beyond a 'mere carnival' parody of women and challenge the heart of suppositions about gender in society. Drag, he writes, can,

> take the form of an *incitement to rebellion*. It can express a desire to revolt against the most tyrannical of laws, the 'natural' link between sex and gender. This drag-as-rebellion, strange to relate, can even represent a rejection of the denigration of women's bodies on the basis of lack.
>
> (quoted in Bruzzi, 1997: 165)

If this is the case, and we can think of drag as an interrogation of gender, one that breaks the link between biologically determined categories and socially constructed conceptions of sex, then female impersonation may constitute a rebuttal of prescriptive roles and an exploration of alternative genders and sexualities. As we have seen, there is a large body of work that puts momentum behind the argument that comic inversion can be a political force, so why not extend it to include drag? If we accept this argument, then we would also be able to apply it, as some Shakespearean critics have done already, to the 'progress narrative'. In this revised version, Shakespearean cross-dressing is not simply explained by 'holiday humours', but is a politicized investigation of gender hierarchies that questions the inferiority of women at a time when the assumption of male superiority was overwhelming. Drag is the vehicle of this investigation as it focuses the attention on the sartorial symbols of gender and recontextualizes them in a way that might lead us to question their cultural power.

The most radical and influential theorist of drag has been the American critic Judith Butler, whose work touches on cross-dressing by way of a larger argument about the fluidity of gender identities. Butler's position can be broadly characterized as 'anti-essentialist' in that she argues for a concept of gender that is not built on a foundation of biology or other predetermined generative categories, but one that is continually 'iterated' through the 'performances' of gender required by culture. Thus we make our gender by performing the expressions that are culturally characteristic of it. 'In this sense, gender is always a doing, though not a doing by a subject who might be said to preexist the deed', she writes; 'there is no gender identity behind the expressions of gender; that identity is performatively constituted by the very "expressions" that are said to be its results' (Butler, 1990: 25). It should be noted that 'gender identity' is not identical to biological sex, but rather the gender with which the subject identifies him or herself, irrespective of their anatomically prescribed or medically understood gender. Traditional feminist responses to drag and cross-dressing, claims Butler, have viewed it as either degrading to women, or as 'an uncritical appropriation of sex-role stereotyping from within the practice of heterosexuality' (Butler, 1990: 137). Rather than arguing the politics of drag from the point of view of drag relying on a discrepancy between the biological sex of the performer and the gender that is being performed, Butler insists that there are three categories at work: 'anatomical gender, gender identity, and the gender that is being performed' (Butler, 1990: 137). As she writes,

> If the anatomy of the performer is already distinct from the gender of the performer, and both of those are distinct from gender of the performance, then the performance suggests a dissonance not only between sex and performance, but sex and gender and gender and performance.
>
> (Butler, 1990: 137)

This concept of drag is one in which the various categories that are confused, mixed, and invoked in cross-dressing demonstrate the non-essential nature of gender:

> *In imitating gender, drag implicitly reveals the imitative structure of gender itself – as well as its contingency.* Indeed, part of the pleasure, the giddiness of the performance is in the recognition of a radical contingency in the relation between sex and gender in the face of cultural configurations of causal unities that are regularly assumed to be natural and necessary.
>
> (Butler, 1990: 137–138, original emphasis)

Drag may therefore be said to reveal that gendered social discourse has no tenable foundation, even if the performer is unaware of the broader implications of their act. However, as Butler concludes, there is no simple test or rubric that determines whether acts of gender parody are subversive, or simply images that have been 'domesticated and recirculated as instruments of cultural hegemony' (Butler, 1990: 139).

While the politicization of drag has not entered the world of comedy to the extent that it exists in the gay, lesbian, and transsexual communities, the themes of 'imitative' gender and gender contingency have been dealt with by performers like the US comedian Sandra Bernhard and the British comedian Eddie Izzard. Clearly neither of these performers wears drag in the conventional sense, but both use their performances to draw attention to the politics of sartorial choice and the gendered assumptions of dress. Both resist the application of prefabricated definitions to label their sexuality, preferring to use their comedy as a means of questioning the validity of labels. Bernhard, who refuses to allow either her performances or sexual orientation to be easily categorized, has been described by

Camille Paglia as a 'drag queen . . . [who] can defend herself without running to grievance committees. Whether lesbian or bisexual, she accepts and respects male lust without trying to censor it' (Paglia, 1994: 140). Izzard describes himself as a 'male lesbian transvestite', a convolution consistent with his routines that are not so much surreal, the usual epithet he attracts, as a cut and paste of the found objects of the media age. Izzard often wears women's clothes on stage, but his representation of sexuality follows much the same principle of choice and assemblage as his act, creating a gender role that does not conform to pre-existing definitions. Izzard says, 'People say, "Why don't you change your clothes at half-time?" Why? Do footballers do this? I'm not a drag act. This is not about the clothes, it's about the comedy and I just do whatever I want' (Izzard *et al.*, 1998: 61).

MARRIAGE

While a notion of femininity is the principal allusion at the heart of cross-dressing and drag, 'real' women are excluded from this important comic motif. A commonly held objection, as formulated by Lucy Fischer, is that transvestite comedy 'privileges the male and claims his dominance even when woman is apparently there', noting also the absence of central women in both comic cinema and in theoretical discussions of the genre, which is 'particularly bizarre given the origins of the mode in female fertility rites' (Fischer, 1991: 62, 63). Aristophanes' *Lysistrata* (412 BC) is the earliest extant play to give significant speaking roles to women, and possibly the first in Western literature. Its plot involves a group of Athenian women who occupy the Acropolis and go on a sex-strike in order to force their husbands into peace negotiations with Sparta. Lysistrata and her group are politically motivated and outspoken women who ransom the state into seeing sense. However, this is not an argument for their emancipation. As Lauren K. Taaffe tells us, the central conceit of *Lysistrata*, a role-reversal that places women in masculine positions (and vice versa), only serves to draw out the subordination of women:

> The integrity of male identity is kept whole, while the absurdity of women in public life is played up. The play confirms and celebrates an ordered

sense of gender identity in which male is stable and female is unstable, in need of control through marriage. Finally, the convention of male actors in female roles ensures that masculinity is always present on stage, even when all the characters are female.

(Taaffe, 1993: 51)

The representation of women in *Lysistrata* is largely symptomatic of the representation of woman in Western comedy as a whole, where she is relegated to a generic purpose, the butt of a joke, or a caricature to be presented by men in drag. Susan Carlson writes that,

In the comic plays populated by women, two features proscribe what comedy's women can be: a basic inversion and a generally happy ending. To understand these two aspects of comic structure is to understand the limitations of comic women. Women are allowed their brilliance, freedom, and power in comedy only because the genre has built-in safe-guards against such behavior.

(Carlson, 1991: 17)

Women are therefore used for two reasons: to provide an hysterical vision of the world-turned-upside down, and to enable male order to be re-established through the subjugation of women in marriage. This would certainly be the most satisfactory way to explain the absolute transformation of Katherine in Shakespeare's *The Taming of the Shrew* (1593–94) from a 'shrewd ill-favoured wife' (Shakespeare, 1989: 1.2.59), to a compliant woman who argues that a husband should be 'thy lord, thy life, thy keeper / . . . thy sovereign' (Shakespeare, 1989: 5.2.146–147). Kate's volatile behaviour is permissible in the context of comedy because it is both temporary and necessary if it is to be finally overcome. The play's characterological incoherence is explained because comedy's view of women is formulaic. It is entirely appropriate that the first wife we meet in the play who conforms to Petruchio's ideal ('My husband and my lord, my lord and my husband / I am your wife in all obedience' (Shakespeare, 1989: Induction, 2. 104–105)), is a male, the page Bartholomew in disguise, underlining the extent to which play-acting and male fantasy override anything like the realistic portrayal of women (Leggatt, 1998: 121).

Marriage could be described as the main reason for the participation of women in comedy, as well as one of the primary conditions under which men and women are seen to interact. Marriage also serves as the conclusion towards which traditional comic narrative inevitably moves, a cultural symbol of the harmonious symmetry and the resolution of troubles. In addition, female characters in comedy are outstandingly susceptible to ideological versions of the male concept of women, largely defined in terms of their suitability for marriage. Particularly common is the representation of women as either virgins or whores, with little room for ambiguity. In the early modern period the official discourse of marriage held that the domestic arena was a microcosm of the state, with the husband the head of the household just as a monarch rules over his people. While this trope of domestic government epitomizes a harmonious ideal, numerous treatises on the proper conduct of husbands and wives also suggest that marriage was a precarious undertaking where 'adultery and whoredom' were ever-present dangers to marital harmony (Newman, 1991: 20). In comedy, women's reputations are forced to negotiate the opposing poles of subordination and infamy. The courtesans of Roman comedy, for example, traditionally belonged to the *hetaerae*, a class of foreigners who enjoyed some freedoms but were denied citizenship and generally considered aliens. As an outsider, the courtesan's sexual services were acceptable, although she remained culturally egregious. In order to become a Roman, the plot demands her transformation, and the reform of her sexual behaviour and ethnic identity. Terence's *Eunuch* (161 BC) features such a device, in which the discovery of the slave Pamphila's true identity clears the way for her marriage to the young Athenian aristocrat Chaerea. However, before the news of the marriage, Chaerea, thinking his beloved beyond his reach, switches places with a eunuch servant, enters her house and rapes her. Chaerea's pride in his fortune and pleasure in his escapade is not censured by his family or peers, aside the mildest chastisement for rascally behaviour. Rather, as the title suggests, the play diverts attention from the issue of rape to consider the comic improbabilities of a eunuch's sexual performance. That Chaerea and Pamphila are eventually married supposedly negates the crime against her, and confirms for us the view that women are either married or legitimate sexual targets.

A similar formulation is found in the comedy of the early modern period, where a woman's acceptance is determined by the sexual status she has in the eyes of men. The sexual defamation of Hero in *Much Ado About Nothing*, for example, results in her supposed death, which can only be reversed by a symbolic resurrection brought about after her name has been cleared. Similarly, the tragi-comic *The Winter's Tale* sees the accused Hermione reborn after her innocence is assured after a period of sixteen years; while Thomas Middleton's *A Chaste Maid in Cheapside* (1613) features Moll Yellowhammer's resuscitation while laid in her coffin. In these cases, women are wrongly accused of improper sexual conduct, an accusation that demands the highest penance that strict social codes allow. To all intents and purposes, Hero, Hermione, and Moll die, and remain dead until the slander against them has been disproved. Only when the meanings that men attach to women have been redefined, may the women be reborn and returned to their places as faithful wives and chaste servants of their husbands.

The citizen comedies of the Jacobean era are particularly well stocked with prostitutes and they generally conform to the image of the fallen woman as a diseased monster. They also serve a moral function, being used to tempt and chastise the prodigal, or being married off to a usurer, as is the case at the end of Middleton's *A Trick to Catch the Old One* (*c.*1605), or David Lord Barry's *Ram Alley* (1608), both examples of comic *contrapasso* where the villain is delivered a deliciously ironic punishment befitting the nature of his crime. There are occasional variations on this theme where the prostitute turns out to have a heart of gold, but, as Alexander Leggatt writes, 'None of the attempts to complicate the conventional opposition of chaste maid and vicious whore really amounts to much: they are all minor effects, frequently uncertain and apologetic' (Leggatt, 1973: 109).

In Middleton and Dekker's city comedy *The Roaring Girl* (*c.*1611), we are presented with a radical exception to proscribed female roles in the unusual character of Moll Cutpurse. Also known as Mary Frith, Moll defies all the conventions of acceptable female behaviour yet retains her unimpeachable chastity. Mary Frith was a real person who began to dress as a man and inhabit the London underworld in the early seventeenth century. Such a unique character occupies a singular position in the play, which seems continually to struggle to know what to do with her and can think of her only as a confusing thing. The first discussion of her by Sir Alexander Wengrave makes this clear:

> It is a thing
> One knows not how to name: her birth began
> Ere she was all made. 'Tis woman more than a man,
> Man more than a woman, and – which to none can hap –
> The sun gives her two shadows to one shape;
>> (Middleton and Dekker, 1994: 1.2.128–132)

It is easier for the men having this conversation to believe that Moll is the victim of a bizarre birth defect, than accept a woman wearing men's clothing. While over forty plays used the convention of women cross-dressed for the purposes of disguise between 1603 and 1619, including *The Roaring Girl* in the character of Mary Fitzallard, it is important to remember that Moll is resolutely *not* in disguise (Stuart, 1993: 31). Her attire flaunts indeterminacy and taunts male opinion. This liminal relationship to categories of definition is further underlined by her mobile relationship to the city, living in several homes at once, and slipping, 'from one company to another like a fat eel / between a Dutchman's fingers' (Middleton and Dekker, 1994: 2.2.206–207). That Moll does not really belong in her own play, is accentuated by the fact that instead of following comedic convention and donning female attire to marry at the end of act 5, she vows to stay single and to remain always dressed as a man. Moll's exclusion from the resolution grants her leave to comment on patriarchy's orthodox views of women. Challenging the female role in marriage, she declares that,

> I have no humour to marry. I love to lie o' both sides o'th' bed myself; and again, o' th'other side, a wife, you know, ought to be obedient, but I fear me I am too headstrong to obey, therefore I'll ne'er go about it . . . I have the head now of myself, and am man enough for a woman; marriage is but a chopping and hanging, where a maiden loses one head, and has a worse i'th' place.
>> (Middleton and Dekker, 1994: 2.2.36–45)

Moll sees marriage as a resignation of her liberty, losing her 'head', her virginity, or at least, sexual integrity, to a man, who then becomes the 'head' of the household.

In Congreve's *The Way of the World*, as in much Restoration comedy, the heroine is apparently contradictory. It may be worth reminding ourselves that the Restoration saw the first actresses perform in theatres, which must have changed the dynamic of the representation of the sexes considerably in contrast to the singularly male population of the Elizabethan and Jacobean stage. Restoration heroines must at once prove their virtue, but also run dangerously close to compromising it through demonstrations of wit that are the foundation of her desirability. This fear is best articulated by Pinchwife in William Wycherley's *The Country Wife* (1675) who declares, 'he's a fool that marries, but he's a greater that does not marry a fool. What is wit in a wife good for, but to make a man a cuckold' (Wycherley, 1996: 1.1.388–390). Near the end of Congreve's play, Millamant, pursued shrewdly and ardently by Mirabell, makes a series of demands, requests that must be satisfied if she is to be his wife. These include,

> liberty to pay and receive visits to and from whom I please; to write and receive letters, without interrogatories or wry faces on your part; to wear what I please; and choose conversation with regard only to my own taste; to have no obligation upon me to converse with wits that I don't like, because they are your acquaintance; or to be intimate with fools, because they may be your relations. Come to dinner when I please; dine in my dressing room when I'm out of humour, without giving a reason. To have my closet inviolate; to be sole empress of my tea table, which you must never presume to approach without first asking leave. And lastly, wherever I am, you shall always knock at the door before you come in. These articles subscribed . . . I may by degrees dwindle into a wife.
>
> (Congreve, 1997b: 297)

At first sight, these privileges look like an attempt to retain independence within marriage, remaining the mistress of her affairs and the gatekeeper of her own private space. Yet they also suggest an attempt to avoid the necessary familiarities of married life, and to retain the formality of court-ship. 'What seem like provisions by Millamant for freedom and power', writes Pat Gill, 'are endeavours not to extend her prerogatives but to freeze time, to remain eternally the same' (Gill, 1994: 121). Thus Millamant tries to avoid the pitfalls of established matrimony characterized by the surly companionship and open infidelities of the older generation that surrounds them.

The complaint that marriage is a form of servitude is certainly what hangs over the portrayal of husbands and wives in many of the popular television comedies of recent decades. Many prominent British sitcoms, including *Whatever Happened to the Likely Lads?* (1973–74), *Bless This House* (1973–76), *George and Mildred* (1976–79), or *Keeping Up Appearances* (1990–95), show marriage as the site of tension between down-to-earth men and pretentious women. A wife's role is to thwart her husband's attempts to act 'naturally', usually defined as drinking, gambling, or going to football matches, whilst encouraging middle-class aspirations and the restraint of childish impulses. The sitcom wife is overly socialized and rigorously abstemious in answer to her husband's perpetual appetite for sensual pleasure. She is formed by consumerism, is unreasonably materialistic, status-obsessed, and concerned with the artificialities of etiquette, whereas her husband believes himself to be unpretentious, relaxed in his identity, dismissive of any person or situation that does not allow him to 'be himself', such as vicars, family gatherings, Conservative politicians, and his boss. Female characters have repeatedly been given the role of joyless authority figures in these shows, wives who are simultaneously mothers to their infantilized husbands. 'Women are forced by sitcom to be the establishment', writes Frances Gray. 'This is clear from innumerable sitcoms in which female absence is the condition that permits male individuality by liberating them from the confines of the family "norm"' (Gray, 1994: 84). This would be the case in shows such as *Steptoe and Son* (1962–74), *Porridge* (1973–77), *Dad's Army* (1968–77), *Yes, Minister* (1980–88), or even a supposedly 'alternative' sitcom like *The Young Ones* (1982–84), where the absence of women helps to emphasize the eccentricity, individuality, uniqueness, and strong characteristics of male characters, who are 'all free to be what they so enjoyably were, precisely because there were no women around to "spoil things" with common sense' (Gray, 1994: 84). This threat is built into the marriage of Bob and Thelma in *Whatever Happened to the Likely Lads?*, which, argues Maggie Andrews, continually makes an issue of 'the boundary between adulthood and lad that Bob is constantly crossing and re-crossing' in continual fear of provoking his wife's ire (Andrews, 1998: 57). Bob's bourgeois lifestyle, nurtured by Thelma, is continually troubled by contact with his friend Terry, whose stint in the army, bachelor life, and unapologetically working-class values amount to the freedom Bob has renounced for his steady job and holidays in Spain. Marriage is therefore the embodiment of lost liberty and denuded proletarian authenticity: 'a comedy of entrapment within the rigid and class-based social structure' (Gray, 1994: 83). The confines of wedlock were treated differently in a generation of sitcoms that emerged from the USA in the 1990s, whose attitude to marriage was one of straightforward avoidance. Shows such as *Seinfeld* (1989–99), *Friends* (1994–2003), and *Frasier* (1993–2004), have no apparent faith in the ability of relationships to last, and all have protagonists who remain resolutely single and inept at maintaining romantic partnerships. What seems to keep them this way is their residency in cities like New York and Seattle as opposed to the suburbs, and a fear of ending up like their parents, such as *Seinfeld*'s unspeakable Frank and Estelle Costanza, themselves a re-rendering of the married couples of 1970s sitcom.

It is perhaps not remarkable that marriage often equals imprisonment in modern comedy, given that marriage is no longer a prerequisite for sexual activity. But even in traditional comedies that conclude with a marriage, the promise of heterosexual sex does not necessarily override or foreclose the sexual mutability that may have gone before. Not all aspects of sexuality are simply carnival deviations permissible prior to their inevitable incorporation into monogamous heterosexual 'normality'. Stephen Orgel and Valerie Traub argue that the sexual identity of the boy players of the Shakespearean stage had erotic significance beyond the structure of the fiction in which they appeared, an erotic significance that spoke to 'homosexual' desires within the audience. Similarly, drag acts reference elements of sexual identity that are neither neatly assimilated into the idea of comic inversion nor disarmed by their self-definition as comic performances. However, it should be noted that in the vast majority of cases, sexual adventurism applies to men only. As we look back over comedy's treatment of gender and sexuality, we must conclude that versions of female sexuality that explore the configuration of women's identity and desire beyond a handful of stereotypes are still severely lacking.

4

THE BODY

Man consists of two parts, his mind and his body, only the body
has more fun.

Woody Allen

'The comic hero, by his very nature,' writes Maurice Charney, 'needs to declare himself the patron of everything real, physical, material, enjoyable, and the enemy of all abstractions, moral principles, seriousness and joylessness. This is a matter of basic allegiance to the life force' (Charney, 1978: 160–161). If the comic hero is a sensualist, then his or her main ally in hedonism is the body. The body in comedy is the medium through which humanity's fascination with its instincts and animal nature is explored. The comic body is exaggeratedly physical, a distorted, disproportionate, profane, ill-disciplined, insatiate, and perverse organism. Any *Tom and Jerry* cartoon exemplifies this extenuated corporeality in its parade of bodies that mutate, disassemble, reconfigure, and suffer endless punishment while refusing to die. Comic heroes are often disproportionate caricatures themselves, excessively fat or ludicrously thin like Laurel and Hardy, myopic and fragile like Mr Magoo, or elastic like Rowan Atkinson and Jim Carrey. We might also say that the comic body privileges the facts of physicality over the ideal of the physique, and its functions over poise, however those ideas might be structured at any particular historical moment. Jerry Seinfeld once said that conventionally attractive people do not make good stand-up comedians, as the audience distrusts beauty in comedy and wants their clowns to be imperfect. An ideal of physicality must exist against which the comedian can be found lacking, thereby reassuring an audience that comic substance will be found in departure from those ideals.

BEAUTY AND ABJECTION

In Western culture, the human body is subject to discourses and regulatory regimes that form and instruct it according to an ideologically driven idea of how it should appear and how it may be properly used. A key theme is its divided nature, capable at once of stunning beauty and grace, and also disease and foul excretions, like a temple built over a sewer. The idealization of beauty in the West has one root in the Platonic system that understood the contemplation of physical perfection as a necessary step on the course to absolute knowledge. In *The Symposium* (*c*.371 BC), Socrates encourages his friends to use beauty as a ladder to the truth, urging them,

> to begin with examples of beauty in this world, and using them as steps to ascend continually with the absolute beauty as one's aim, from one instance of physical beauty to two and from two to all, then from physical beauty to moral beauty, and from moral beauty to the beauty of knowledge, until from knowledge of various kinds one arrives at the supreme knowledge whose sole object is that absolute beauty, and knows at last what absolute beauty is.
>
> (Plato, 1951: 94)

Beauty in human beings is therefore a partial reflection of an absolute beauty that is good, virtuous, and metaphysically inseparable from truth. For Aristotle, the kernel of beauty lay in perfect orderliness, writing that 'the chief forms of beauty are order and symmetry and definiteness' (quoted in Synott, 1993: 80). A parallel idea can be found in the Old

Testament's book of Isaiah: 'The carpenter stretcheth out his rule; he marketh it out with a line; he fitteth it with planes, and he marketh it out with the compass, and maketh it after the figure of a man, according to the beauty of a man' (44: 13). Classical architecture used perfect bodily proportion as a divinely gifted template for the organization of buildings, especially temples, a principle developed by the Roman architect and military engineer Vitruvius (*fl.* first century AD). In Book III of his *De Architectura*, he writes, 'No temple can have any compositional system without symmetry and proportion, unless, as it were, it has an exact system of correspondence to the likeness of a well-formed human being' (Vitruvius, 1999: 47). A beautiful human form is therefore the perfect compositional template, its symmetry and proportion constituting an embodiment of the divine plan.

Concomitant with the idealization of beauty is a cultural insistence on mastering the body, and making it conform to ideas of deportment and appropriate behaviour, regulating its functions and odours according to what is considered acceptable, and what must be suppressed as crude or bestial. Norbert Elias, whose ground-breaking work *The Civilizing Process* (1939) demonstrated how a concept of the body, and the appropriate way of managing it, lay at the heart of ideas like refinement and civilization, argues that one of the principal means of governing bodily manners has been through the introduction of shame. Feeling ashamed, or developing a heightened sense of delicacy about nakedness, table manners, flatulence, and other 'unpleasant' biological facts, requires disciplining bodily functions to fit the codes of etiquette and avoid being shunned. As the rules of bodily discipline become increasingly refined, a parallel sense of the primitive and brutish is created in its wake:

> The greater or lesser discomfort we feel toward people who discuss or mention their bodily functions more openly, who conceal and restrain these functions less than we do, is one of the dominant feelings expressed in the judgement 'barbaric' or 'uncivilized'. Such, then, is the nature of 'barbarism and its discontents', or, in more precise and less evaluative terms, the discontent with the different structure of affects, the different standard of repugnance which preceded our own and is its precondition.

> (Elias, 1978: 58–59)

By demonstrating our disapproval of standards lower than our own we construct a category of barbarism against which we guarantee our elevated level of civility.

It is against these ideals of beauty and manners that physical comedy is produced. Put simply, comedy strategically bypasses civility to return us to our body, emphasizing our proximity to the animals, reminding us of our corporeality and momentarily shattering the apparently global imperatives of manners and beauty. Obscene, sexual, or taboo humour is predicated on an understanding of the socially tolerable body that it perverts in order to provoke laughter. Yet this does not amount to an authentic moment in which we are granted a genuine and unmediated experience of our material selves, but rather a discovery of the body through the contravention of civility. Out of the concept of bodily order, then, emerges the comic body.

One idea that may help us understand the place of the body in comedy is the notion of 'abjection'. This concept, developed in its most familiar form in the psychoanalytic criticism of Julia Kristeva, contemplates those things which repulse or nauseate the subject but which do not utterly belong outside him or her. In his study of abjection in stand-up comedy, John Limon describes it as 'a psychic worrying of those aspects of oneself that one cannot be rid of, that seem, but are not quite, alienable – for example, blood, urine, feces, nails, and the corpse' (Limon, 2000: 4). The abject is an ever-present site of horror and fascination that pollutes the self, because the self partly consists of it. This is most clearly characterized by the actual body, which will eventually die. As Kristeva writes:

> The corpse, seen without God and outside of science, is the utmost of abjection. It is death infecting life. Abject. It is something rejected from which one does not part, from which one does not protect oneself as from an object. Imaginary uncanniness and real threat, it beckons to us and ends up engulfing us.
>
> (Kristeva, 1982: 4)

We see here that the abject is a physical reality that cannot be defeated through the simple application of additional layers of cultural refinement. In Limon's terms, the abject 'worries' at us, refusing to be sublimated, never entirely forgotten and implicated in one's very existence. Abjection may explain why 'sick', morbid, or scatological humour, or comedy that involves violence and pain, is so popular. Such examples go straight to the worry, addressing the inescapable bodily facts of existence that are elided by manners. We know that medieval Biblical drama often incorporated elements of farce and burlesque, styles that use violence, physical predicaments, and scatology in their comedy, as if indicating a desire to raise the troubling issues of finitude in the presence of God. By foregrounding the functions of what Bakhtin calls the 'lower bodily stratum', the genitals, the anus, urine, excrement, and excrescences, and invoking the abject body as a risible concept to be laughed at rather than feared, its power of horror may be lifted and our fear of decay and degeneration alleviated. But the comedy of abjection is also a confirmation of the frail foundation of civility, locating subjectivity within material existence, acknowledging the weakness of the body and the omnipotence of filth, and raising themes that are impermissible elsewhere.

THE GROTESQUE

The grotesque could be described as an embodiment of the abject. A form of humorous monstrosity devised for satiric purposes, the grotesque marries the repulsive and the comic, as in the paintings of Hieronymus Bosch (c.1450–1516) or George Grosz (1893–1959), or even in the spirit of pantomime dames. Retrospectively applied to the decorative arts of Ancient Rome, the term originally referred to an imaginative combination of the real and the fantastic, and especially an unnatural or stylized distortion of organic nature in stark contrast to the regularity of classical order (Vitruvius himself complained about it bitterly). 'Grotesque' was a term initially reserved for the visual arts, but later extended to include anything across the arts that contained elements of the ridiculous, the horrifying, and the bizarre. The grotesque is a form of exaggerated and ambivalent social commentary produced by the violent clash of opposites, especially those that are comic and terrifying, existing in a state of unresolved tension. The site of the grotesque clash is the human body, resulting in deeply ambiguous and divided reactions to the horror of corporeality and oneself as an organism. Mr Creosote, the diner from the 1983 film *Monty Python's The Meaning of Life*, might serve as an example. Here is a man so gluttonous that his eating causes him to vomit torrentially – until he ultimately explodes after eating an after-dinner mint. Mr Creosote survives but finds himself ripped apart and looking down at his exposed ribcage and enlarged heart. As viewers, we are amused by the absurdity of the spectacle, and appreciate its poetic justice. But the image is also unnerving and disgusting, a visceral rendition of a body destroyed by its own appetite and made to witness what it has done. It is the unresolved nature of this scenario that gives the grotesque its particular force. The grotesque, then, is a humorous mode that aims to produce an ambiguous feeling pitched somewhere between pleasure and disgust.

By far the most notable author of grotesque comic fiction is François Rabelais (*c*.1494–1553). Rabelais's stories of the giants Gargantua and Pantagruel follow them through a series of absurd adventures and grotesque scenarios that celebrate physicality by means of an unremitting obsession with it. Rabelais's giants and their companions engage in a continual round of eating, drinking, defecating, urinating, sweating, copulating, and passing wind. They are insatiately anal, oral, and phallic monstrosities whose sexual and scatological openness hopes to release the world from pathological inhibitions and the stress of maintaining manners. What they champion is unruly, desiring, animal existence in the face of censorious and ascetic intellectualism. The proximity of humanity to the body is continually stressed from the moment Gargantua's mother goes into labour in Book I. His birth is prefaced by a characteristic case of mistaken identity:

> A while later she began to groan and wail and shout. Then suddenly swarms of midwives came up from every side, and feeling her underneath found some rather ill-smelling excrescences, which they thought were the child; but it was her fundament slipping out, because of the softening of the right intestine – which you call the bum-gut – owing to her having eaten too much tripe . . .
>
> (Rabelais, 1955: 52)

The confusion of the baby and bodily waste is symptomatic of the text's substitution of subjectivity with materiality, and its paralleling of cognitive categories with bodily functions. However, Gargantua and Pantagruel are not only representatives of an infantile or hedonistic id, but rather the medium through which Rabelais launches satirical attacks on a range of subjects including education, medicine, the ecclesiastical establishment, monastic life, and the nature of justice. Rabelais deployed his satire in the Erasmian fashion, ridiculing pretension and ignorance by saturating it in exaggeration. For Mikhail Bakhtin, of course, Rabelaisian grotesque was the purest possible manifestation of the popular-festive folk identity. Arguing that Rabelais's novels reject any kind of boundaries between the mannered and disciplined body and the procreative, alimentary, corpulent, or offensively abject body, Bakhtin claims that Rabelais's 'grotesque realism' demonstrates 'the body in the act of becoming' (Bakhtin, 1984: 317). 'We find at the basis of grotesque imagery', he writes, 'a special concept of the body as a whole and of the limits of the whole. The confines between the body and the world and between separate bodies are drawn in the grotesque genre quite differently than in the classic and naturalistic images' (Bakhtin, 1984: 315). The grotesque body is not a closed system defined by clear limits, but a body that reaches out beyond its boundaries and interacts with the world on a sensual level:

> The stress is laid on those parts of the body that are open to the outside world, that is, the parts through which the world enters the body or emerges from it, or through which the body itself goes out to meet the world. This means that the emphasis is on the apertures or the convexities, or on various ramifications and offshoots: the open mouth, the genital organs, the breasts, the phallus, the potbelly, the nose. The body discloses its essence as a principle of growth which exceeds its own limits only in copulation, pregnancy, child-birth, the throes of death, eating, drinking or defecation.
>
> (Bahktin, 1984: 26)

The grotesque is therefore a vivid celebration of inter-connectedness, growth beyond death and the continuity of existence, where the body is triply significant as a representation of ideal community, the embodiment of festivity, and interpenetration and connection of the human body with the universe. Once expressed in these terms, it is clear why some critics have accused Bakhtin of a 'romanticization and heroization of the body' (Critchley, 2002: 51).

A modified example of Rabelaisian grotesque would be Shakespeare's Sir John Falstaff, a figure for whom the celebration of corporeality always takes place within the context of a direct challenge from the disciplines of order and self-control. Falstaff is often thought of as a representative of carnival, his Eastcheap antics standing in contrast to the statesmen and soldiers of the rest of the play; *1 Henry IV*, by thus giving its reprehensible characters a dramatic status equal to its aristocratic ones, can be viewed as 'the first play in English to find major imaginative stimulus in the disreputable' (Rhodes, 1980: 99). Falstaff, a liar, a glutton, a coward, and the consort of prostitutes and thieves, is a symbol of degeneracy and perpetual leisure. In a passage where Prince Hal mimics his father's displeasure, we can see how Falstaff is imagined as a parade of meats:

> There is a devil haunts thee in the likeness of an old fat man; a tun of man is thy companion. Why dost thou converse with that trunk of humours, that bolting-hutch of beastliness, that swollen parcel of drop-sies, that huge bombard of sack, that stuffed cloak-bag of guts, that roasted Manningtree ox with the pudding in his belly . . .
>
> (Shakespeare, 1989: 2.5.407–413)

Falstaff's body is a distempered creation stitched together from organs, fluids, and edibles: 'In each image,' writes Neil Rhodes, 'Falstaff is . . . a barrel of diseases or a horn of plenty which can be exchanged and replenished at any moment' (Rhodes, 1980: 109). For Anne Barton this constantly changing grotesque makes Falstaff a hero, the descendant of a long line of characters who 'detest war and the ideals of military glory':

> They are healthily sceptical of the pretensions and promises of politicians, and their own unabashed physicality makes them insist on recognizing and celebrating man's links with nonhuman creation. Monstrous egoists and opportunists, they are enemies of society, but also its raffish saviors.
>
> (Barton, 1985: 133)

In the final battle at Shrewsbury, Falstaff carries a bottle of wine where his pistol should be, falsely boasts of killing Percy, feigns death to avoid injury, and ultimately lives, enacting the image of a carnival resurrection, and a life-affirming, if dishonourable, alternative to politics and warfare. As C. L. Barber writes: 'Whereas, in the tragedy, the reduction is to the body which can only die, here reduction is to a body which typifies our power to eat and drink our way through a shambles of intellectual and moral contradictions' (Barber, 1963: 213).

Just as the end of *2 Henry IV* sees Falstaff banished from Hal's presence on pain of death, and kings and carnival strictly kept apart, after the renaissance the grotesque appears to have been relegated to the margins of comedy. Neo-classical comedies of manners privileged wit over physical humour, and revised concepts of authorship meant that the onus fell increasingly on performers to respect the integrity of the text to the detriment of clownish improvisation. At this stage, we can see comedy draw away from the body and privilege plot, evinced by the plays of Molière, Marivaux, Etherege, Wycherley, and others, whose plays accelerate action verbally while simultaneously decreasing the space it occupies.

Although the grotesque withdrew from comic literature, it enjoyed a coincidental rise in the graphic arts, especially as caricature. Caricature, taken from the Italian, *caricare*, meaning 'to overdetermine' or 'to overload', isolates particular features in its subjects, the nose, say, and enlarges, alters, or otherwise manipulates them in order to emphasize particular qualities of appearance. Charles Baudelaire (1821–67), who wrote a series of articles on caricature, considered it an example of the '*comique absolu*', or absolute comic, because its grotesque distortions had the power to shock the viewer into an awareness of the ironic duality of life, 'at once embodying and exposing the division and fragmentation of the modern subject, representing and revealing the terrifying and exhilarating otherness of modern experience' (Hanoosh, 1992: 4). Caricature operates according to the principle that we are all potentially monstrous, as the prominently exaggerated or altered features communicate the identity of the subject depicted, and so caricature makes us identifiable by deforming us. Caricature is most readily associated with satire, with physical distortion commensurate to the vices of its targets. William Hogarth (1697–1764), the painter and engraver best known for his series of 'modern moral subjects' *The Harlot's Progress* (1732), *The Rake's Progress* (1733–35), and *Marriage à la Mode* (1743–45), used caricature in a distinctly literary fashion, adopting an Horatian tone that belittles greed and hypocrisy. Caricature's place in national political debate was also established in the eighteenth century, where cartoonists used it as a means of transforming targets into the personification of their vice. For Freud, the pleasure in caricature is derived from its ridiculing of political figures, even when the image itself is unsuccessful, 'simply because we count rebellion against authority as a merit' (Freud, 2001: 105). Martha Banta, who has studied nineteenth- and twentieth-century caricature in both the USA and Britain, sees it as a subtle but powerful forum for establishing the nature of normality. The questions that were being asked in these cartoons, she writes, dealt with 'essential (essentialist) concerns', which 'broke through as a series of pictorial enquiries: "What is 'English'?" "What is 'American'?" "What is 'civilized'?" "What is 'barbaric'?" and the most basic anxiety of all, "Where can we feel safe?"' (Banta, 2003: 23). Caricature helped to mediate these questions by pictorially imagining the 'other' and making it monstrous or ludicrous in order to service the anxieties of the white, urban middle-class readership of magazines like *Punch* and *Life*. Pictorial caricature is therefore a shorthand that uses elements of the human figure as a means of conveying a complete set of ideologically correlated ideas.

SLAPSTICK

'Slapstick' is generally understood as physical humour of a robust and hyperbolized nature where stunts, acrobatics, pain, and violence are standard features. Broad comedy of this type has been around since Aristophanes, but the form known as slapstick came into being as practically the sole condition of comedy in early American cinema, along with the keen artistry of performers like Charlie Chaplin, Buster Keaton, and Harold Lloyd, and the enterprise of legendary producers like Mack Sennett. Slapstick is a perfect example of the way in which genres are shaped by the media that present them, as moving pictures remained soundless until 1926, forcing humour to be silent and visual. For Stanley Cavell, the technological considerations of early film were absolutely central to the comedy it produced for two reasons:

> First, movie performers cannot project, but are projected. Second, photographs are of the world, in which human beings are not onto-logically favoured over the rest of nature, in which objects are not props but natural allies (or enemies) of human character. The first necessity – projected visibility – permits the sublime comprehensibility of

Chaplin's natural choreography; the second – ontological equality –
permits his Proustian and Jamesian relationships with Murphy beds and
flights of stairs and with vases on runners on tables on rollers.

(Cavell, 1979: 36–37)

Thus we are presented with the projected body that draws attention to its
surface and movements, placed among a world of things over which
it cannot claim superiority. Ironically for silent film, the term 'slapstick'
is onomatopoeically derived from the sound made by the wooden paddles
clowns used to beat one another with in the burlesque touring theatres.
These were in turn versions of the inflated sheep bladders filled with dried
peas that accompanied clowns on the early modern stage, themselves an
echo of the tools used to beat the ritual scapegoat in ancient ritual. The
scapegoat, a person onto whom the accumulated evils of the community
were transferred prior to his or her expulsion, might be a useful way of
understanding the hero of slapstick comedy. Slapstick comedians generally
played the role of outsider, such as Chaplin's Tramp character, awkward,
if physically gifted, loners who found themselves swimming against the
tide of modern living. Thrust as innocents into a world they had never
apparently encountered before, their hapless bodies suffered the misfortunes that might befall us in our daily lives so that we did not have to. Yet
however often the body was assaulted it was largely indestructible,
rendering concern or sympathy for a character's pain irrelevant. In this
sense, slapstick may be said to represent a socially acceptable expression
of masochism, as the viewer takes no sadistic pleasure in the pain induced,
or, perhaps, a liberation from the compulsion to empathize.

The slapstick protagonist is continually prone to attack through either
a bodily revolt or loss of self-control, or from an external source that aims
to dismantle his dignity. In both slapstick movies and the cartoons they
inspired, the body is utterly malleable and infinitely resourceful. At the
heart of slapstick is the conceit that the laws of physics are locally mutable,
that the world can rebel against you, or that a person can be suddenly
stripped of their ability to control their environment or anticipate how it
will behave. The body in slapstick is often at odds with the mind that
inhabits it, suggesting a dysfunction of the mind/body dualism that
emphasizes the dividedness of human experience. Slapstick historian Alan
Dale reads the beleaguered hero as a reconfiguration of the relationship

between the mind and the body that has been a feature of conceptions of humanity since classical antiquity. 'One of the central elements of . . . theology,' he writes,

> the debasing effect of the body on the soul – enables Christians to overcome this discord only by denying and finally getting rid of the body, whereas slapstick achieves accord here on earth by a comic concession to the body at its most traitorous. Both of these stand in contrast to the pagan approach of the Olympic Games, in which athletes attempt to achieve a perfect union of body and will. These three ritualistic approaches form a gamut: Christianity seeks eternal triumph over physicality after life; Olympians seek by means of the body a temporal triumph that will be remembered long after the athlete's prowess has faded; slapstick seeks a temporal acceptance of physicality by a cathartic exaggeration of its very limitations.
>
> (Dale, 2000: 14)

As well as being a vicarious outlet for cruelty, then, the humour in slapstick may also help to reconcile us to a body that obstructs the will and insubordinately thwarts desire.

As slapstick is where the body meets the world of things, it is suitably fascinated with objects. By examining the identity and utility of things and playing with the space they occupy, their dimensions, properties, and cultural significance, the body's relationship to the external world is made strange. Typical gags might involve disproportionate sizes, the animation of the inanimate, the slowing down or speeding up of events, the personification of objects, and the reversal or rejection of linear cause and effect that allows things to be re-contextualized or entirely reused. This belongs to a rich tradition of clowning. The most popular routines of the famous Regency comedian Joseph Grimaldi (1778–1837) were the ones where he turned cheeses into a coach, and produced a hussar's uniform out of a coal scuttle, a cloak, and a muff. The Swiss-born clown Charles Wettach, better known as Grock (1880–1959), speaks tellingly of his relationship to objects in his autobiography: 'Ever since I can remember,' he wrote, 'all kinds of inanimate objects have had a way of looking at me reproachfully and whispering to me in unguarded moments: "We have been waiting for you . . . at last you've come . . . take us now, and turn us into something different"' (quoted in Welsford, 1935: 309). Laleen Jayamanne sees the clown's ingenuity as 'an unsevered link between perception and action', that amounts to the ability to think with the body rather than the more familiar coordinates of subject–object relations, resulting in 'the capacity to make correspondences, the perception of non-sensuous similarities across incommensurables', such as eating an old shoe as if it were a gourmet meal, as in Chaplin's *The Gold Rush* (1925) (Jayamanne, 2001: 189). The idea that the slapstick gag represents an interruption of conventional knowledge is put forward by Donald Crafton, who argues that the utility-turned-unpredictability of slapstick gags amounts to a rupture in the linear process of understanding. 'One way to look at narrative', he says,

> is to see it as a system for providing the spectator with sufficient knowledge to make causal links between represented events. According to this view, the gag's status as an irreconcilable difference becomes clear. Rather than provide knowledge, slapstick misdirects the viewer's attention, and obfuscates the linearity of cause–effect relations. Gags provide the opposite of epistemological comprehension by the spectator. They are atemporal bursts of violence and/or hedonism that are as ephemeral and as gratifying as the sight of someone's pie-smitten face.
>
> (quoted in Jayamanne, 2001: 185)

Rather than taking events and shaping them into coherent order, slapstick events treat the world as if it were capricious, unpredictable, and suddenly explosive. To think of a gag as an 'irreconcilable difference' is to emphasize its incompatibility with our understanding of how the world normally works. Slapstick, then, opens up the possibility of the world becoming inhospitable and strange to us.

A useful way to consider slapstick is through the work of Henri Bergson. Bergson, as discussed in Chapter 1, believed that human beings exist in a state of continual ambient awareness of the animated 'vital spirit' of themselves and others, and that when a situation causes vitality to be obscured and the 'humanness' of humans is lost or denuded, comedy is born from the sudden eclipse of life. 'The comic', he says, 'is that side of a person which most reveals his likeness to a thing, that aspect of human events which, through its peculiar inelasticity, conveys the impression of pure mechanism, of automatism, of movement without life' (Bergson, 1980: 117). This especially includes moments where judgement is overridden by the actions of the body, such as any situation 'that calls our attention to the physical in a person, where it is the moral side that is concerned' (Bergson, 1980: 93). One of Chaplin's greatest films, *Modern Times* (1936), is extremely Bergsonian in this sense. Set against a backdrop of mass labour and industrialization, the unique and individuated body is contrasted with the faceless and automated machines of production-line capitalism. Essentially, the film asks whether it is possible for individuals to retain their sympathetic emotional qualities when their lives are controlled by the working week and subservience to heartless institutions. The film opens in a steel mill with Chaplin performing repetitive tasks at a conveyor belt, an action that penetrates him so deeply he adopts its automated twitch. While, from one perspective, this is a dark comment on the reification of labour, from a Bergsonian view it represents comedy in its purest form, insofar as 'The attitudes, gestures and movements of the human body are laughable in exact proportion as the body reminds us of a mere machine' (Bergson, 1980: 79). The mechanized body is one of the key symbols of the film, with two set pieces built around the uncomfortable meeting of body and technology. The first features an automatic feeding device to which the worker is strapped and fed by robot arms, with the result that the meal is smeared all over Chaplin's face and clothes, as if he were an infant in a high chair. The second involves Chaplin's co-worker becoming stuck in the enormous cogs of a machine while Chaplin tries to feed him his packed lunch. In both predicaments, something particularly human – mealtimes, with their array of cultural meanings, rituals, and strong associations of need and sensual enjoyment – is marred through the intervention of something senseless, inorganic, and utterly unsympathetic. In fact, missed or frustrated meals recur throughout the film, underlining the extent to which the Tramp is always at some distance from bodily satisfaction and that the availability of sustenance is tied to economic success. The alternative to faceless frustration is the 'gamin', Paulette Goddard, Chaplin's wife at the time, who plays a feral female representative of authentic vitality. After her father is killed in a labour riot, the gamin comes under the protection of Chaplin who instantly assumes the overlapping roles of protector and uncertain mate. An absence of obvious sexual interest was typical of Chaplin's character, and his thin cane and voluminous trousers have been taken as symbols of waning male sexuality (Segal, 2001: 432). For the new couple, respite from privation takes priority over sex. In a scene in which Chaplin takes the job of night watchman in a department store, the new couple enact a fantasy of leisure and plenty, characterized by their unfettered access to the luxury goods on the shelves. A similar bourgeois 'green world' idyll is conjured up as the couple sit on the lawn of a suburban bungalow and imagine life as middle-class pastoral, where the trees are heavy with fruit and the cows deliver fresh milk. Ultimately, Chaplin's slapstick in *Modern Times* is the dumbshow of bodily cravings against social denial.

THE FEMALE BODY

The golden age of Hollywood slapstick was not a golden age for female comedians. Women rarely performed the kind of stunts their male co-stars were famous for, and were used instead as figures of erotic interest, sentiment, or ridicule. The prolific producer of silent-era slapstick, Mack Sennett, imposed rules for the use of women in his films according to a descending scale of hilarity that held that old maids were the funniest targets, mother-in-laws were second, but that it was absolutely forbidden to make a mother the butt of jokes for fear of alienating the audience (Dale, 2000: 92). Women who occupy the roles traditionally considered sacrosanct by men, the romantic partner or the mother, could not be represented as either physical or humorous in slapstick cinema, whereas the old or the unattractive could. This is because 'Comedy positions the woman not simply as the object of the male gaze but of the male laugh – not just to-be-looked-at but to-be-laughed at – doubly removed from creativity' (Gray, 1994: 9). The objectification of the female body in comedy is clearly evident: as the reward that awaits the hero, or in jokes as the primary locus of taboo, an imaginative source for the proliferation of obscene and visceral humour that focuses on sexual attributes.

As we have seen in Chapter 3, a woman's place in comedy has been defined by either her sexual identity or her availability for marriage. As a result, comedy engages in the repetition of negative stereotypes. Women are handed the role as the 'handmaid of laughter, not its creator', in television programmes such as *The Benny Hill Show* (1969–89), where women actors wore 'revealing frocks . . . an expression of perpetual surprise (men are so clever/naughty) and a special way of moving that jiggles as many separate parts of the body as possible while covering the minimum ground' (Gray, 1994: 21–22). 'What unites the narrow spectrum of female types in the traditional modes of popular British comedy', writes Lorraine Porter, 'is their *a priori* definition by physicality and sexuality: the tart or dumb blonde by her over-determined sexuality, or *her excess of sexual difference*, and the tyrant or spinster by her absolute asexuality, or her *lack of sexual difference*' (Porter, 1998: 70). While we might consider that the 'spinster' or other unattached women often represent a more sinister threat of sexual otherness, rather than the negation of sexual difference, Porter correctly identifies the female body as the genesis of woman's place in comedy. A sanitized version of this phenomenon results in the virtual elision of the female body in the pleasant but asexual Anglo-Saxon wives and mothers of early TV sitcom. In 1952, for example, the American show *I Love Lucy* was unable to refer to pregnancy, even though its star Lucille Ball was heavily pregnant and the show featured an episode in which Lucy was delivered of a son (Horowitz, 1997: 30). In this, the treatment of women speaks not so much of a risible and caricatured sexuality, but a fear of female corporeality and the reproductive consequences of male fantasy. There is a long tradition of conduct literature and etiquette books instructing women to control themselves and to be deferential and remain largely silent. Wit in women, while common, was to be discouraged and seldom displayed in public. John Gregory's *A Father's Legacy to His Daughters* (1774), warns that,

> Wit is the most dangerous talent you can possess. It must be guarded with great discretion and good nature, otherwise it will create you many enemies. Wit is perfectly consistent with softness and delicacy; yet they are seldom found united. Wit is so flattering to vanity, that they who possess it become intoxicated, and lose all self-command.
>
> (quoted in Burney, 1998: 341–342)

One is reminded of Jane Austen's Emma, sharply reprimanded by Mr Knightley for making a joke at the expense of the meek Miss Bates (Austen, 1987: 368). Gregory's equation of wit and vanity repeats a misogynist commonplace that women are prone to narcissism, and will succumb to it as easily as Eve did to temptation. The connection between humour and moral suspicion has existed since the earliest writings of Christianity. Joseph Addison mentions that he once heard a sermon on the belief that 'laughter was an effect of original Sin, and that Adam could not laugh before the Fall' (Addison and Steele, 1979, vol. 2: 237), while Baudelaire held that 'Laughter is Satanic; it is therefore profoundly human' (Baudelaire, 1992: 148).

Women have been systematically denied the power to be funny for a number of cultural reasons. First, there is the often-repeated opinion that women are not as naturally funny as men due to the belief that comedy is boisterous and aggressive and therefore temperamentally unsuited to women. A product of this is the perceived ghettoization of women's comedy and the belief that female comedians only discuss 'women's' themes – relationships, shopping, and menstruation, for example – whereas male topics are thought to be unbounded and therefore to have universal appeal. Second, if women are seen to be funny, then this is thought to be a function of the genre rather than the qualities of the performer; as Leslie Ferris says, 'the more symbolic . . . "woman" becomes, the less she herself is and can be culturally creative' (Ferris, 1990: 29). In addition, female roles in comedy are limited and limiting and are often misinterpreted as evidence of the limitations of female humour. Most pervasively, comedy is culturally associated with a degree of sexual openness deemed inappropriate for women. Regina Barreca, who writes extensively on women and comedy, remarks that,

> In communities throughout the world . . . women who tell jokes are regarded as sexually promiscuous. The connection between humor and sexual invitation is made up of many links, among them the thought that it takes a certain 'fallen' knowledge to make a joke. Women in some Greek and Italian villages, for example, are considered less than virtuous if they so much as laugh aloud in mixed company. Only old women – or women who are somehow outside the sexual marketplace – are permitted to make lewd remarks.
>
> (Barreca, 1991: 50)

The laws of deportment, etiquette, and sexual propriety, therefore, traditionally discourage woman's humour as it gives cause to suspect their virtue. Not only is the intimation of forbidden knowledge worrying, the effect of laughter upon the body is a contributing factor to the equation of women's humour with sexual threat as it dissolves good posture, contorts the face, causes physical abandon, and produces a loud noise. Laughter shatters the illusion of women as quiet and poised and reveals them as fearfully bodily and biological creatures. The horror of the exposed female body threatens to debase the ideals of beauty and romance transposed onto women by men, as in Jonathan Swift's poem, 'The Lady's Dressing Room' (1730), where the voyeur Strephon cannot believe 'Such order from confusion sprung / Such gaudy tulips raised from dung' (Swift, 1967: ll. 141–142).

The comic abjection of the female body and its foundation in cultural gender bias can be seen in Middleton's *A Chaste Maid in Cheapside*. This city comedy features a scene in which three puritan 'gossips' attend a christening, get drunk, and wet themselves. Gail Kern Paster has shown how this scene, and the play's overall attention to urinary tropes, draws together a number of patriarchal assumptions about female vocal, sexual, and physical 'incontinence' that locate cultural views of femininity in medical discourse. Early modern theories of sexual difference believed that men were essentially 'hotter' than women, accounting for their supposedly active dispositions and external genitals. By contrast, women's relative coolness and supposedly idle lives made them considerably more 'watery'. This medical fact produced a series of associations connecting women with water, especially the sense of a woman as a vessel whose impermeability or otherwise was an allegory for her chastity and moral value. The puritan gossips are therefore 'leaky' women: their unrestrained talking shows their lack of discipline, reinforced by their weak bladders. 'The female characters of *A Chaste Maid in Cheapside*', writes Paster, 'reproduce a virtual symptomatology of woman which insists on the female body's moisture, secretions, and productions as shameful tokens of uncontrol' (Paster, 1993: 52). That much of the play's action takes place during Lent draws out the iniquities of character by emphasizing their total lack of abstinence and physical denial.

There are, of course, generations of female comedians who, while often uncelebrated, have been extremely able physical comedians, as Morwenna Banks and Amanda Swift's history of women in music hall shows (Banks and Swift, 1987). Of the better-known examples of physical comedy written and performed by women, Jennifer Saunders's *Absolutely Fabulous* (1992–96) has been the most prominent of recent years. In the double act of Patsy and Edina, Saunders personifies the pretensions of the publicity and fashion industries and the hedonism and egomania that accompany them. The grotesque physicality of this pair, who are so penetrated by the contradictory and dictatorial demands of fashion that they have become utterly misshapen, ridicules the beauty worship to which they are slavishly subject, which in its purest form demands that women subjugate their bodies entirely to become demure and non-corporeal. The satire of the industry and its vacuous beliefs is literally performed on the bodies of the women, in the garish and poorly judged clothes they wear, in Patsy's promiscuity, Edina's immaturity, and the pair's drunkenness. All of these are clearly forms of incontinence, castigating women for cherishing inappropriate ideas about themselves and inverting the generation gap. Women are not being universally chastised, however, but rather these individuals are singled out for the vacuity of their values and their eleva-tion of ideals that ask women to conform to unattainable standards of perfection. *Absolutely Fabulous*'s frank discussion of sex and the body is part of a broader movement of women writers who 'are creating characters who realize a much fuller and more troublesome range of bodily possibilities' (Carlson, 1991: 250). Certainly in the 1990s, a number of female comedians came to prominence whose material dealt with their identity as women, and the social, physical, and sexual expectations placed upon them. Jo Brand, for example, has built a career on challenging male views of appropriate female behaviour, and media that perpetuate a male ideal of femininity:

> if a Martian come down to earth and just had to watch telly and read magazines to find out what women were like he'd think that they were all blonde and 25 with big tits. . . . Also he would think they were never rude and always looked nice, they always deferred to men, a lot of the time. Obviously there are exceptions to that on television, but I'm saying that's the general essence of it. So I like not to be like that.
>
> (Brand, in Wagg, 1998: 122)

A number of performers and television shows testify to the fact that comedy written and performed by women successfully occupies a mainstream position in twenty-first-century popular culture. However, this cannot be simply accredited to tastes changing over time, but is rather the fruit of the concerted political efforts of feminism since the 1960s. Clearly, comedy is not immune to ideology but is saturated in it. As we have seen, the use of the body in comedy is derived from normative cultural concepts of bodily deportment and physical beauty. As such it reflects dominant ideological codes, but, as Jo Brand and others demonstrate, it can also be the vehicle that challenges them through parody, satire, and ridicule. In order to better understand the ideological battles that have been fought through humour, we should therefore consider further the relationship of comedy to politics.

5

POLITICS

Humour is an aspect of freedom, without which it cannot exist at all.

Malcolm Muggeridge

One of the less traumatic but nevertheless noticeable effects of the events of 9/11 was the voluntary moratorium on humour that immediately followed it in the American media. As a reaction to the horror of that day, intolerance for joking and an extreme sensitivity to the inappropriateness of laughter became a further way of emphasizing the extent of the tragedy. Some commentators were even moved to see 9/11 as occasioning the demise of certain types of humour: *Newsday* columnist James Pinkerton, for example, wrote of it as a 'crushing defeat for irony, cynicism and hipness' in America. Certainly, there were none of the poor taste jokes that followed hard on the heels of the Challenger disaster (1986), the King's Cross fire (1987), or the explosion on the Piper Alpha oil platform (1988). In the weeks after the attacks, the nightly talk shows of David Letterman and Jay Leno stayed off the air, and when they returned they returned without their opening monologues. The suspension of humour was temporary, of course, and within two weeks the 26 September issue of the satirical newspaper *The Onion* carried the headline 'God Angrily Clarifies "Don't Kill" Rule'. Shortly thereafter an explicit command to laugh again came from Rudolph Giuliani, the Mayor of New York, who during a charity opening in October told the crowd 'I'm here to give you permission to laugh. If you don't I'll have you arrested'. In time, the ability to laugh became symbolic of the resilience of Americans in general and New Yorkers in particular, with the freedom to laugh being held up as a defining feature of American democracy. Laughter – the pleasure, dissent, and first amendment freedom to express oneself freely that it seems to assume – came to stand in opposition to the fundamentalist dogmas and joyless religious strictures that were believed to characterize those responsible for the attacks. The US comedian Lewis Black, whose routine takes the form of exasperated commentaries on current affairs, puts this idea most succinctly when he argues that 'the terrorist is a person without humour at all' (Black, 2003). Can we therefore imply a direct connection between the freedom to laugh and the right to live freely? What is the nature of the relationship between humour and freedom, and how does politics colour the world of comedy?

The philosopher of humour, John Morreall, believes that a resilient sense of humour is an intrinsic defence against tyranny. 'The person with a sense of humour can never be fully dominated, even by a government which imprisons him,' he writes, 'for his ability to laugh at what is incongruous in the political situation will put him above it to some extent, and will preserve a measure of his freedom – if not of movement, at least of thought' (Morreall, 1983: 101). A similar idea is found in Lord Shaftesbury's *Sensus Communis* (1709), where humour offers a release from the frustrations of social justice, and a nation's appetite for comedy is formed in direct proportion to the degree of political oppression at work there. Discussing the 'spiritual Tyranny' of Italy, he writes that,

> the greatest of Buffoons are the ITALIANS: and in their Writings, in their freer sort of Conversations, on their Theatres, and in their Streets, Buffoonery and Burlesque are in the highest vogue. 'Tis the only manner in which the poor cramp'd Wretches can discharge a free Thought. . . . The greater the Weight is, the bitterer will be the Satir. The higher the Slavery, the more exquisite the Buffoonery.

> (Shaftesbury, 1988: 141)

Arguably the notion of humour as an inherent expression of freedom is over-romanticized, as it is possible to imagine circumstances or hardships where laughter offers no comfort. Nevertheless, humour has been demonstrably policed or punished by many governments who see it as a form of subversion. In 1737, the fear of ridicule prompted Sir Robert Walpole to introduce the Licensing Act censoring the theatre and its satirical attacks on his government. Hitler 'was so wary of the danger of humour to the Third Reich that he had special "joke courts" set up for, among other things, punishing people who named their dogs and horses "Adolph"' (Morreall, 1983: 102). In 1935, the Berlin cabaret comedian Werner Finck was imprisoned in a concentration camp for a sketch that parodied limitations on the freedom of speech under Nazism (London, 2000: 34). In Soviet Russia it was strictly forbidden to publish satire that criticized the party or its officers – a crime punishable by imprisonment in labour camps. In the United States during the 1950s, the investigations of Senator Joseph McCarthy's House Committee on Un-American Activities, established to root out communist sympathizers and treasonous plots at home, drove humorists underground for fear of blacklisting or incarceration. In 1952, Charlie Chaplin's uncontroversial film *Limelight* was singled out for McCarthyite suppression. *Limelight* was apolitical, but the millionaire Chaplin, who had always retained his British citizenship, was thought to hold too much sympathy for the workers. Chaplin was refused re-entry to the United States until he had appeared in front of the Immigration Board of Inquiry to answer questions of a 'political nature and of moral turpitude'. He resettled in Switzerland and returned to the USA only once to receive an Oscar in 1972 (Boskin, 1997: 75–76). Comedy might side with freedom of speech in these examples, the laughers against paranoid and totalitarian regimes, but it is equally the case that comedy can be used in the service of repression, what Christopher Wilson calls the 'cryptic conservative' (Wilson, 1979: 226). The denigration of difference found in racist and sexist comedy, for example, reinforces and validates a discourse of power that relies on the systematic humiliation of targeted groups to secure its own sense of identity. In Albert Cook's view 'comedy is approval, not disapproval, of present society; it is conservative, not liberal' (quoted in Carlson, 1991: 15). Clearly Cook overstates the case, but the question of what we laugh at, and how it is censored or condoned by authority, is a highly politicized area, and comedy can be the site of manifest ideological struggle.

COMEDY AND THE STATE: *FROGS* AND *BRASS EYE*

In its earliest form, comedy engages with politics and the state. Aristophanic comedy, for example, frequently defames identifiable Athenian public figures and derides their policies. Each of Aristophanes' eleven surviving plays is broadly based on a political theme pertinent to Athenian institutions and democracy, or individuals within the polis. Abuse that we would now consider libellous was a fundamental part of the comedy, with named officials, military officers, and prominent citizens all insulted in considerable detail. Given the level of communal participation with Greek drama and huge attendance at the annual Dionysia, Aristophanic dissent would have been widely broadcast. This responsibility or function appears to have constituted part of the identity of the playwright, and textual evidence makes it clear that Aristophanes imagined himself as the conscience of the people, exposing corruption and political misman-agement and ridiculing the offenders. As the Chorus of *The Acharnians* says,

> He'll carry on impeaching
> Every abuse he sees, and give much valuable teaching,
> Making you wiser, happier men. There won't be any diddling
> Or flattery or bribes, or any other kind of fiddling,
> Nor will you drown in fulsome praises, such as all the rest
> Bestow on you: he thinks his job's to teach you what is best.
>
> (Aristophanes, 1973: 78)

In all likelihood, this passage was written in response to events of the previous year, when *The Babylonians*, a play now lost, resulted in Aristophanes' probable conviction for slandering the city in the presence of foreigners. This is probably the first time that comedy claims for itself the privilege of licence, or of operating somewhere beyond the law.

The nature of political commentary in Aristophanes tells us that his work was conceived as a deliberate intervention in affairs of state. At the beginning of his career, Athens was a powerful and democratic city under the leadership of the popular and charismatic Pericles (*c.*495–429 BC). Athens's success threatened its neighbour Sparta, and in 431 BC, the two cities entered into wars that would last intermittently for twenty-six years and result in the eventual surrender and subjugation of Athens in 405 BC. Throughout this period, Aristophanes maintains consistently pacifist sentiments and opposes the hardships and loss of freedoms brought about by lengthy conflict. Towards the end of his career, condemnations and caricatures of politicians are coupled with a new nostalgia for pre-war Athens and a lament for the depletion of the ideals of democracy. In *Frogs*, written only a few months before the final surrender of the Athenians, the god Dionysus is found mourning the recent deaths of the tragic poets Euripides and Sophocles, and lamenting the absence of good writers in Athens. With his servant Xanthias, he disguises himself as Heracles and travels into Hades to recover Euripides and return him to the upper world. In the underworld he presides over a poetical contest between Euripides and the older poet Aeschylus, and on balance, the high-minded, old-fashioned verse of Aeschylus is preferred over the newer style of his opponent, and so Aeschylus is reinstated to life. *Frogs* therefore insists upon the importance of literature to the spiritual life of the nation and affirms conservative poetical values. We can see this as an assertion of the centrality of drama to political and cultural discourse, with comedy as the only literary form able to enlist fantasy and disregard boundaries as a means of retrieving lost ideals.

Even though Aristophanic comedy is immersed in political themes, it is not necessarily a vehicle for dissent and political change. Criticism is divided between those who read his comedy as a profound engagement with the issues of public life and those who see him as a professional comedian getting laughs from the humiliation of authority figures. To support this latter argument, critics point to the context of comic drama within the two annual dramatic festivals, the Lenaea and the Dionysia. Adopting an approach familiar from new historicism, the argument cites the loosening of manners and mores during festival time, and the ritualistic centrality of raillery and abuse in the *kômos* as the principal motivation for apparently political humour. The insults of Aristophanes are therefore part of the same formula as phallic worship and farce, and their political relevance is a secondary effect. In Stephen Halliwell's words, this 'is not an evasion of standards, but rather an institutionalized and culturally sanctioned exemption from them' (Halliwell, 1984: 19). According to this view, comedy is by its very nature as politically impotent as it is apparently permissive.

The question of whether or not comic form automatically reduces the political potential of comic content was raised by the scandal involving the broadcast of a *Brass Eye* special about the media treatment of paedophiles. The programme, shown on Channel 4 on 26 July 2001, co-written by and starring Chris Morris, was a parody of a current affairs programme. Each episode in the series satirized media sensationalism, poor journalism, and the irresponsibility of tabloid practices in a jaded media market. To expose the culture of sound bites and ubiquitous celebrity comment, politicians and media figures were asked to condemn fictional issues or make on-camera appeals in support of invented campaigns. In this episode, the singer Phil Collins was filmed wearing a 'Nonce Sense' campaign T-shirt, while the radio DJ Dr Fox was seated in front of a dead shellfish, saying, 'Genetically, paedophiles have more genes in common with crabs than they do with you or me . . . it is scientific fact'. Reactions to the programme were fierce. Culture Secretary Tessa Jowell spoke directly to the head of Channel 4 to voice her concern and try to elicit a guarantee that the programme would never be repeated. The Home Office minister Beverley Hughes branded the show 'unspeakably sick', and the Home Secretary David Blunkett called it 'not remotely funny', although both later admitted that they had not seen it. The *Daily Mail* columnist Simon Heffer described it as 'the most grievous breach of taste I have ever witnessed on TV, and a programme that only a small proportion of the psychologically sick could have found enjoyable' (*Daily Mail*, 28 July 2001). While upholding the channel's right to free speech, the Independent Television Commission forced Channel 4 to broadcast an apology two months later, after it became clear that *Brass Eye* was the most complained about television programme in British broadcasting history. Clearly, it was the opinion of many that comedy had no business with such a topic.

This particular episode of *Brass Eye* was conceived in response to the reductive and incendiary treatment of the issue of paedophilia in the British media. The summer of 2000 saw a series of riots involving anti-paedophile protestors distressed at the presence of men they believed to be abusers living freely in their neighbourhoods. Such actions were in part inspired by the *News of the World* that had been running a series of articles naming alleged offenders and including some details of their whereabouts. As its target was the media, the issues of paedophilia themselves were not considered, which undoubtedly proved to be the most provocative characteristic of the programme, as it appeared to lack any sentimentality for children, or reiterate any familiar expressions of the sanctity of childhood as a state of being. Neither did it temper its attack on publicity-hungry celebrities and politicians with an unambiguous statement in support of the victims of abuse. Many read these omissions as signs of fatal ambiguity, but one suspects that demands for overt statements of authorial intent, or the refusal to permit one aspect of the issue to be separated from the others, would have been unnecessary had the programme treated a different subject. As co-writer David Quantick said, 'I think a lot of people complained because it had the word paedophilia in the title and that a lot of complaints seemed to be related to a show that didn't go out' (*Guardian*, 30 July 2001). Much of the opposition to the show now seems to have been sparked by its enunciation of a culturally volatile term that provokes instantaneous suspicion every time it is uttered outside of the condemnatory discourse designed by the media. Yet for the representatives of the government to comment on the content of a comedy show demonstrates that not all issues are covered by a blanket licence granted to comedy to speak out of turn.

SATIRE

Brass Eye's defence was built entirely upon its self-identification as satire. While claiming that something is satirical does not exempt it from criticism, it does imply a parodic tone that should not be confused with a straightforward correspondence with the author's views. Satire exists all over the media, and is by no means an exclusive effect of comedy, but it is the most directly political of comic forms and the one that has caused the majority of censorious government interventions. Satire aims to denounce folly and vice and urge ethical and political reform through the subjection of ideas to humorous analysis. In the best instances, it takes its subject matter from the heart of political life or cultural anxiety, re-framing issues at an ironic distance that enables us to revisit fundamental questions that have been obscured by rhetoric, personal interests, or realpolitik. Michael Moore's satirical documentary on US gun laws, *Bowling for Columbine* (2002), had an enormous impact on audiences and provoked fierce criticism from conservative groups, and Moore was both cheered and booed when the film received an Oscar. As for fictional works, Stanley Kubrick's 1963 film, *Dr Strangelove; or, How I Learned to Stop Worrying and Love the Bomb*, is an excellent example of how satire can ask a question that has been dismissed by the establishment as naive, but remains absolutely crucial to the future of humanity. Kubrick's film is the story of an insanely paranoid American general who initiates a nuclear strike on Russia to prevent them from stealing his bodily fluids. Russia launches a counter-strike, and both governments try to recall their planes, but one gets through and drops a hydrogen bomb on the Russian base at Laputa, named for one of Swift's lands in *Gulliver's Travels*. *Dr Strangelove* therefore asks a perfectly reasonable but basic question: are our military leaders and their fail-safe systems competent enough to prevent a devastating nuclear accident? In the character of the psychotic ex-Nazi Strangelove, it asks if we can really trust the individuals who lurk behind the anonymity of government departments. In the wake of President John F. Kennedy's assassination, Columbia Pictures delayed releasing the film to avoid accusations of anti-Americanism. When the film did appear, the following disclaimer appeared over the title sequence:

> It is the stated position of the United States Air Force that their safeguards would prevent the occurrence of such events as are depicted in this film. Furthermore, it should be noted that none of the characters portrayed in this film are meant to represent any real persons living or dead.
>
> (Kubrick, 1964)

The second half of this statement is not entirely true: President Merkin Muffley was based on Presidential candidate Adlai Stephenson, and the monstrous Strangelove is a concoction of various German scientists whom the USA had adopted in a Faustian bargain, among them the V2 rocket designer Werner von Braun. But the film's insistence on its fictionality reveals its acute sensitivity to the potential volatility of its satire.

Satire is derived from the Latin *satura*, which means 'medley', or 'hotchpotch', and also described a type of dish, alluding to its origins in country festivals and at feasts. Satire is usually categorized according to the influence of two ancient Roman writers, Horace (65–8 BC) and Juvenal (AD *c*.60–*c*.136), often thought of as stylistically opposite. Horace is gentler, concerned with maintaining moral standards and wishing to improve the ethics of his contemporaries by suggesting a point of equilibrium between extremes. His tone is amused but not scornful, appearing as a spokesperson for common sense, judicious balance, and 'telling the truth with a smile' (Horace, 1959: 34). Central to Horatian satire is a series of contrasts between the country and the city, ideal and practical ethics, and the demands of public and private life. In all these, Horace is a poet of moderation, reserving his censure for those who desire more than they need. Satire VI is typical of Horace's modesty and rejection of the ambition that 'pulls everyone forward, chained to the wheels / Of her gleaming chariot'. Addressing an imagined politician, whose own status is derived from his father's elevated position, Horace, the son of a freed slave, says,

> . . . if nature arranged for us all
> After a specified time to begin life all over,
> Choosing parents who suited our fancy, I'd stick with mine
> And not go for persons distinguished in public life.
> The mob would think me insane, but you, perhaps, wouldn't,
> For being unwilling to shoulder a load I'm not used to.
> If I took on this role, I'd straightaway need some more money,
> Need to receive more callers and endure more visits,
> Take this friend along or the other, and never go out
> By myself or get out to the country . . .
>   . . . In this, and in thousands of other respects,
> I am much better off than you, my dear Public Figure.
>   (Horace, 1959: 66–67)

This sense of balance reflects the poet's own relative investment in the status quo. He was a part of the literary circle gathered around the emperor Augustus' finance minister Maecenas that included Virgil, the poet of the *Aeneid*, a privileged group devoted to the Latinization of Greek poetic forms and the enhancement of Roman poetry. We can also detect the influence of Stoicism, an Athenian philosophical system widely adopted in Rome. Stoicism's chief ethical concern was that humanity live according to the tenets of nature and reason. As all animals have needs befitting their nature, such as the need for food, shelter, and a mate, humanity must live according to these needs, and the actions that nature has prescribed as 'appropriate'. But, as humans are possessed of reason, they can determine the quality of appropriate actions with greater accuracy and consistency than animals, allowing them to move beyond simply answering their needs, and enabling them to act in concert with nature's prescriptions. To act and understand in this way is to act virtuously. Thus, while we can see that Horace is not an explicitly philosophical poet, his satire is concerned with the spiritual well-being of the individual, achieved through individual choices and the reconciliation of self with its place in society.

A century later, the satire of Juvenal suggests that Roman life had changed. Unlike Horace, Juvenal's work was not popular or widely read in his own lifetime, in fact, he was not really 'discovered' until two and a half centuries after his death. Juvenalian satire is the satire of *saeva indignatio*, or savage indignation, the bitter condemnation of venal and stupid humanity. Whereas Horace scolds deviance from an essentially benign human nature, Juvenal starts from the position that vice is at its highest point and virtue has been virtually extinguished. 'When was there ever a time more rich in abundance of vices?', he asks in his First Satire, 'Wealth, in our hearts, is set in the veriest Holy of Holies' (Juvenal, 1958: 21). Juvenal's two most influential satires, Satires III and X, focus on city living and its corruptions. Satire III, 'Against the City of Rome', makes it clear that hypocrisy is necessary for those who wish to prosper:

> What should I do in Rome? I am no good at lying.
> If a book's bad, I can't praise it, or go around ordering copies.
> I don't know the stars; I can't hire out as assassin
> When some young man wants his father knocked off for a price;
> . . .
> I am no lookout for thieves, so I cannot expect a commission
> On some governor's staff. I'm a useless corpse, or a cripple.
> Who has a pull these days, except your yes men and stooges
> With blackmail in their hearts, yet smart enough to keep silent?
>
> (Juvenal, 1958: 35)

Juvenal enjoyed a particular vogue in the eighteenth century when English authors rediscovered satirical models as a powerful form of social commentary. The most influential of these was undoubtedly the complex Irish writer and divine Jonathan Swift (1667–1745). Swift's satire, although difficult to define absolutely, adopts the Juvenalian tone of bitter indignation, appalled by man's inhumanity and the greed and hypocrisy of political and religious factionalism. Swift's misanthropy is voiced through the techniques of irony and parody, deploying an urbane and calming narrative tone to investigate the darkest and most unsettling topics, and using pre-existing literary modes to convey them. This is clearly the technique of *A Modest Proposal* (1729), a short text that outlines a plan to address 'the present deplorable state' of Ireland by selling babies to be eaten as food (Swift, 1993: 2181). *A Modest Proposal* is a parody of the political treatises and pamphlets published in abundance at this time, ventriloquizing the reasonable tone of the concerned philanthropist. 'I shall now humbly propose my own thoughts, which I hope will not be liable to the least objection', writes the urbane narrator, before telling us that,

> I have been assured by a very knowing American of my acquaintance in London, that a young healthy child well nursed is at a year old a most delicious, nourishing, and wholesome food, whether stewed, roasted, baked, or boiled; and I make no doubt that it will equally serve in a fricassee or a ragout.
>
> (Swift, 1993: 2182)

The ethics of cannibalism and degradations of the Irish under colonial English rule are entirely flattened amidst the logical computations and analyses of the humanitarian benefits outlined by the pamphleteer. Such appalling obliviousness to the variance between the 'modest' proposal and the consequences of selling one hundred thousand children a year for meat is typical of the cognitive distance Swift exploits in order to expose his targets to maximum contempt. Like Juvenal, and indeed like *Brass Eye*, Swift offers no counter-argument that can either be concretely identified with the authorial position or be considered socially constructive. This has made his satire appeal to widely disparate groups: both English and Irish nationalists have claimed him as theirs; the Protestant and Catholic churches see him as a defender of their faiths; Marxists read in his satire a withering critique of bourgeois capitalism; and 'despite his association with misogyny', Swift has been celebrated as one of the 'Fathers of Feminism' during Women's History Month in 1996 (Kelly, 2002: 133). 'Satire', he wrote in the preface to *The Battle of the Books* (1704), 'is a sort of glass, wherein beholders do generally discover everybody's face but their own' (Swift, 1984: 104).

'ALTERNATIVE' COMEDY: *COMEDIANS* AND COMEDIANS

In 1971, Granada Television first broadcast *The Comedians*, a simple and enormously popular show that ran for more than fifty episodes and countless repeats. The show is notable because its stars, many of whom had never appeared on television before, came to epitomize a style of stand-up comedy that was vilified in an unprecedented politicization and re-evaluation of comedy that took place in Britain throughout the 1970s and 1980s, known as 'alternative comedy'. *The Comedians* featured a high turnover of routines, edited into a fast-paced package that broadcast each comedian telling only one or two jokes. Most of its performers were seasoned professionals drawn from the privately owned nightclubs and working men's clubs run by the Club and Institute Union (CIU). The comedians of the CIU circuit had an enormous repertoire of formulaic jokes, material that was often sold in bulk rather than written to order, and over which individual comedians had no proprietary rights. Much of this material had an aggressive subtext, expressing in particular racist, sexist, and homophobic sentiments, such as Bernard Manning's: 'There was a plane crashed in Madrid about six month ago, two hundred Japanese on that plane, broke my fucking heart. Six empty seats there was' (Manning, 1993). To a certain degree, the material reflected the context of the performance, as the style suited a rapid non-narrative delivery – practical means when coping with large and sometimes difficult crowds for whom the comedian was simply one more act on a variety bill.

In response to comedy of this kind came a new sensitivity to the practice of joking and its implicit politics. 'Alternative' comedians rejected the easy racism and fast delivery of the gag comic, replacing it with revised form and content. One of the first and probably the most articulate formulation of these issues is found in Trevor Griffiths's play *Comedians* (1976). Griffiths, a playwright whose work tackles questions of class consciousness and left-wing politics, examines the power of comedy to support prejudices and instruct people in bigotry through a group of men attending a night class for aspiring comedians about to perform their debut show. Griffiths alludes to the construction of jokes in his choice of characters, a proportion of whom belong to the groups stereotyped by the CIU-style comedians: two Irish labourers, a Jewish club-owner called Sammy Samuels, Gethin Price, a British Rail van driver, and a walk-on part by a lost Pakistani called Patel. Their tutor is Eddie Waters, the retired 'Lancashire Lad', a principled Shavian socialist who believes strongly in the transformative power of comedy. After warming his students up with a tongue-twister, 'the traitor distrusts truth', Waters matter-of-factly starts to abuse the Irish, 'flapping hands, stinking of soil and Guinness. The niggers of Europe', before doing the same with Jews, 'Say Jew, say gold' (Griffiths, 1979: 18–19). While his class laugh embarrassedly and shuffle their feet, Waters carries on:

> Negroes. Cripples. Defectives. The mad. Women . . . Workers. Dirty. Unschooled. Shifty. Grabbing all they can get. Putting coal in the bath. Chips with everything. Chips and beer. Trade Unions dedicated to maximizing wages and minimizing work. Strikes for the idle. Their greed. And their bottomless stupidity. Like children, unfit to look after themselves. Breeding like rabbits, sex-mad. And their mean vicious womenfolk, driving them on. Animals, to be fed slops and fastened up at night. (*Long pause.*) The traitor destroys the truth.
>
> (Griffiths, 1979: 19)

This shopping list of prejudice is intended to shock, a deliberate ploy by Waters to warn his students away from the easy targets and lazy jibes of the club comedian. In essence it invokes the spirit of club comedy without the punchlines, exposing it for a lightly sugared bigoted tirade. For Waters, the repetition of prejudice in comedy consolidates ignorance in the minds of the audience by reinforcing it through intolerant laughter. Turning laughter on bigotry is, however, the most positive thing that comedy can do; it should tell the truth, reveal things for what they are, delivering people from the constraints of prejudicial ideologies, to become 'a radical mode of social communication' (Garner Jr, 1999: 133). In this credo, entertainment is secondary to the redemptive and revelatory function of the 'true' joke. 'We work *through* laughter, not *for* it', he says,

"Comedian dares to see
What his listeners shy
away from"

116 POLITICS

It's not the jokes. It's not the jokes. It's what lies behind 'em. It's the attitude. A real comedian – that's a daring man. He *dares* to see what his listeners shy away from, fear to express. And what he sees is a sort of truth, about people, about their situation, about what hurts or terrifies them, about what's hard, above all, about what they *want*. A joke releases the tension, says the unsayable, any joke pretty well. But a true joke, a comedian's joke, has to do more than release tension, it has to *liberate* the will and the desire, it has to *change the situation*.

(Griffiths, 1979: 20, original emphasis)

Comedy retrieves a suppressed truth, but not in purely Freudian terms as a means of keeping larger repressions in their proper place, but as a revolutionary force that liberates people from their fear, interrogates repression, and converts it into positive political energy. 'Most comics *feed* prejudice and fear and blinkered vision', he says, 'but the best ones, the best ones . . . illuminate them, make them clearer to see, easier to deal with' (Griffiths, 1979: 23).

Waters's philosophy contrasts strongly with that of Bert Challoner, a talent spotter for the clubs and the man who represents the way on to the circuit. His advice advocates conformity to the style: 'Don't try to be deep. Keep it simple. I'm not looking for philosophers, I'm looking for comics' (Griffiths, 1979: 33). The abdication of responsibility implied by Challoner's view that 'we're not missionaries, we're suppliers of laughter', or the logic of the argument that jokes are 'only' jokes, is the consumerist fallacy that Griffiths wishes to condemn in this play (Griffiths, 1979: 33). Waters sees a direct relationship between racist humour and the logic of fascism. Recalling a visit to a German concentration camp while in the army entertainment corps ENSA, Waters finds a horrific correspondence between jokes and the brutality of anti-Semitism. 'In this hell-place', he says, he saw 'a special block, "Der Straf-bloc", "Punishment Block". It took a minute to register, I almost laughed, it seemed so ludicrous. Then I saw it. It was a world like any other. It was the logic of our world . . . extended. . . . And I discovered . . . there were no jokes left. Every joke was a little pellet, a final solution' (Griffiths, 1979: 64). In this obscene absurdity, that those incarcerated in a concentration camp should have a special place reserved for further punishment, as if such a thing were possible, he sees the cruelty of the joke and the perversity of the camp are cut from the same cloth, different in degree, but not in kind (Garner Jr, 1999: 141).

Having established the insidiousness of club comedy, one is presented with the problem of what a responsible, inclusive, and liberating comedy might look like. Act 2 of *Comedians* tries to think this through via the performances of the students. Here the theatre audience takes the place of the audience in the club, a device that relocates the theatre patrons and places them in, one imagines, largely unfamiliar surroundings and dares them to laugh at the acts they are about to see. The first student, Mick Connor, appears to follow Waters's advice. His routine is drawn from his background, with material on the Catholic confession, the prurience of priests, and the inconsistencies of sex and faith. Connor seems at least to be confronting his fears, even including a rather standard joke about the IRA, which in his mouth comes across as an anxious gag about stereotypes and the violence that plagues his country. Sammy Samuels, who has already signalled his ambition to play the 'tops', begins his routine in similar fashion with comment on his Jewish upbringing. Seeing Challoner entirely unmoved breaks his nerve and sends him into a routine that targets the Irish, West Indians, feminists, homosexuals, and sexual assault. The Ulsterman George McBrain follows the same path, although his is marked by a deep misogyny that appears in the refrain 'my wife, God, she's a slut'. Samuels and McBrain, predictably, are the only students signed up by Challoner to play the clubs. The centrepiece of act 2, and the entire play, is Gethin Price's routine, a bizarre and aggressive act that owes more to Grock and Antonin Artaud's theatre of cruelty than to Frank Randle, the northern comic he purports to idolize. Price is clearly the most artistically gifted and ideologically motivated of the comedians, yet he produces work that is dramatically out of place in the club setting and stretches the definition of comedy until it is entirely unrecognizable. He enters white-face in denim jacket and boots, '*half clown, half this year's version of bovver boy*' (Griffiths, 1979: 48). The act begins with a piece of mime, setting fire to a violin bow, and crushing the violin underfoot. His first words sum up the violence and frustration that characterize him and his routine: 'Wish I had a train. I feel like smashing a train up. On me own. I feel really strong. I wish I had a train' (Griffiths, 1979: 49). After a complicated series of kung fu exercises, a couple of mannequins are brought on, a male and a female, dressed for a night at the theatre. We imagine them waiting for a taxi as Price enthusiastically greets them, before it becomes apparent that the couple have nothing to say to him: 'Been to the match, have we? Were you at t'top end wi'lads? Good, wannit? D'you see Macari? Eh? Eh? (*Silence.*) P'raps I'm not here. Don't you like me? You hardly know me. Let's go and have a pint, get to know each other' (Griffiths, 1979: 49). Through the disjointed and coarse dialogue, Price conveys the inarticulacy and anger he perceives in the working-class male, marginalized by middle-class society and reduced to expressing himself through violence and sexual aggression; becoming, in fact, a stereotype of the prejudices that define his class. His routine does include two standard jokes, one sexual, one racial, but both are delivered maniacally and to the dummies rather than the audience. In this context, they seem like desperate and pathological symptoms of rage, rather than pleasurable social exchanges. Towards the end of the routine, Price offers the lady a flower:

> Here. (*He takes a flower out of his pocket, offers it to them.*) For the lady. No, no, I have a pin. (*Pause. He pins the flower – a marigold – with the greatest delicacy between the girl's breasts. Steps back to look at his work.*) No need for thanks. My pleasure entirely. Believe me. (*Silence. Nothing. Then a dark red stain, gradually widening, begins to form behind the flower.*) Aargh, aagh, aagh, aagh . . . (*The spot shrinks slowly on the dummies, centring finally on the red stain. PRICE's 'aaghs' become short barks of laughter. Innocence.*) I wonder what happened. P'raps it pierced a vein.

(Griffiths, 1979: 51)

This disturbing image, followed by a simple rendition of the socialist anthem the 'Red Flag', is an explicit expression of the militant subtext of Price's act, where revolutionary politics are confusingly mixed with aggression and sexual threat. While Challoner can only describe it as 'repulsive', Eddie Waters calls it '*brilliant*', but the final discussion between Price and Waters reveals considerable tensions between the two men. Price is full of revolutionary anger, while Waters retains faith in political truth and social redemption. Yet something has been satisfied by Price's iconoclastic performance. Politics, commitment, and the articulation of experience have all been drawn upon to produce a genuine and truthful event. No conventional description would call it comedy, however. There is not one single laugh in the fictional club, and one doubts there are many in the theatre either. Is it possible, then, to have entertaining comedy on these terms?

In 1979, amateur promoter Peter Rosengard set up the Comedy Store in a strip club in London's Soho district. This club proved to be important in the development of modern British comedy as it served as a laboratory for the experiment presciently outlined in Griffiths's play. In Oliver Double's terms, it brought 'a handful of comic revolutionaries together, [and] gave them a stage on which they could learn to be funny' (Double, 1997: 165–166). Alternative comedy was overtly political from the start, informed by a punk ethos that dominated British counter-culture in the mid to late 1970s, it defined itself against the expectations of mainstream performance, and encouraged people to write their own material, set up their own gigs, and perform without the need for agents or the approval of the concert secretaries of the CIU. Looking back across fifteen years of alternative comedy, *Guardian* comedy critic William Cook described its ideals in terms reminiscent of the ethics of Eddie Waters, as a form that celebrated 'similarity, rather than condemning difference. The best of it hits hard and it hurts, but it's philanthropic not misanthropic, a bridge and not a wall. Above all Alternative Comedy reveals, via laughter, something of the real life of the comedian' (Cook, 1994: 16). One of the first casualties of the new comedy was the joke-form itself, which had become guilty by association. Alternative comedy deliberately parodied and derided the idea of 'jokes' as reactionary and dull, as in Peter Richardson and Nigel Planer's anti-joke 'what's yellow and goes into the toilet? Piss' (Sayle, 1988). While many routines now seem hopelessly naive, the movement had the momentum and the talent to bring an entire generation of performers to the attention of the public. Most important was the work it did raising awareness of the prejudice that lurked in much mainstream comedy, and in making audiences increasingly intolerant of it. However, alternative comedy is no longer the iconoclastic force it once was, and has managed to retain only the vaguest of liberal consciences since it became big business and was incorporated into radio and television. The market dominance of the watered down alternative comedy has also had the peculiar effect of allowing comics like Bernard Manning to portray himself as the victim of censorship and martyr to political correctness. Manning's publicity now presents him as the man they could not gag, a modern appropriation of clown who dares to say the unsayable. This is presented as an authentically working-class position, dispossessed by the uptight nanny state: 'Can't stop us laughing can they?', he says in an aside, 'It's the only thing we've got left' (Manning, 1993).

THE END OF LAUGHTER? THREE HOLOCAUST COMEDIES

The self-evidently inappropriate proximity of the word 'comedy' to 'Holocaust' raises a question: are there times when comedy and politics must not mix? While our instincts tell us that comedy has no place in such appalling events, several attempts have been made to treat Holocaust themes within a context that is either structurally or tonally comedic. The results are of course varied, but the interaction of two categories that common sense tells us are diametrically opposed can be extremely interesting, both in terms of what possible benefits, if any, comic elements bring to an understanding of history, and also where the practicable boundaries of comedy's much-vaunted freedom to flaunt taboos might lie. Allusions to the Holocaust have been used by a number of Jewish comedians as an emblem of the limits of bad taste or wrong-headedness many times, suggesting that even thinking about it is fraught with guilt and difficulty. The comically abysmal musical 'Springtime for Hitler' at the heart of Mel Brooks's film *The Producers* (1968), devised to defraud the insurance company with a failed Broadway show, suffers a reversal when it turns out that the theatre-going public *love* Nazi-themed musicals. The fraudsters, the critics, and the Broadway audience are all shown to be appalling philistines. An episode of *Seinfeld* saw Jerry censured by his parents and his girlfriend's father after they were spotted kissing in the cinema during *Schindler's List* (1993). In *Annie Hall* (1977), Woody Allen's character Alvy refuses to see any movies other than the four-hour documentary on Nazi-occupied Paris, *The Sorrow and the Pity*, because 'everything else is such garbage' (Allen, 1977). With this comment he demeans its force by putting Marcel Ophüls's film in the same category as the average Hollywood blockbuster, appreciable according to standard popular criticisms by, for example, the credibility of its plot, the thrilling-ness of effects, and so on. In all three of these examples, the Holocaust is used as the absolute signifier of seriousness contrasted against light-headed concern for entertainment, daily life, and diminutive but nagging desires. The Holocaust acts as a grave reminder against which the self-centredness of the over-privileged modern bourgeois is made utterly risible.

Other attempts at considering Holocaust themes in comedy have been horribly ill-conceived. The American comedian Jerry Lewis directed and starred in a 1972 film entitled *The Day the Clown Cried*, a story about a German circus clown, Helmut Doork, who is arrested for a drunken impersonation of Hitler and sent to Auschwitz. During his incarceration he befriends the children of the camp and performs for them with the hope of bringing some laughter into their lives. At the end of the film he tries to shield them from their fear by leading them to the gas chambers, while, the screenplay says, playing the harmonica like the 'pied piper'. That the film lacked judgement is borne out by the fact that it remains unreleased. Lewis's unfortunate project underlines the extreme difficulty of attempting to treat the subject of the Holocaust without reducing it to banal sentimentality or simply using it as the backdrop for clowning. The problems of the meeting of comedy with content of this kind are obvious. Not only is comedy generically and tonally unsuited to a treatment of the Holocaust, but there is a structural misfit too. Comedy concludes with a standardized happy ending, 'a conscious superimposition of a formal pattern on material that may until the very last moment whirl with turbulence', in Zvi Jagendorf's phrase, but here there no question of such a thing (Jagendorf, 1984: 43).

Let us consider three films that have attempted to do so with varying degrees of success and controversy: Charlie Chaplin's *The Great Dictator* (1940), Frank Beyer's *Jakob the Liar* (1974), based on the novel by East German writer Jurek Becker, and remade in America as a vehicle for Robin Williams in 1999, and Roberto Benigni's triple Oscar-winning *Life Is Beautiful* (1998). While each of these films has a different strategy for dealing with this jarring incompatibility, none of them can resist the implied trajectory of comic narrative as a means of injecting their stories with some optimism and the possibility of future happiness, even if it exists way beyond the final scene. We see this in the equation of laughter with hope, and the implication that comedy is the representative of a caring and inclusive human spirit that cannot be extinguished by fascism. In *The Great Dictator*, set in fictional Tomainia, Hitler look-alike Adenoid Hynkel has risen to power on anti-Semitic policies and by fermenting international unrest. The film contrasts Hynkel's rampant megalomania, revealed in a scene where he performs a delicate ballet with an inflatable world globe, with the parallel story of a humble Jewish barber who returns to the ghetto after several years in hospital suffering from amnesia. Chaplin played both Hynkel and the Barber, and the stories move together in order to bring about a concluding scene in which the Barber, imprisoned for his religion, escapes from a concentration camp and is mistaken for Hynkel just as it is time for him to give a speech. Knowing that his life depends on maintaining the charade, the Barber launches into an impassioned six-minute plea that closes the movie. From his opening words, the speech is resolutely anti-dictatorial: 'I'm sorry, but I don't want to be an Emperor,' he says, 'that's not my business. I don't want to rule or conquer anyone. I should like to help everyone if possible, Jew, gentile, black man, white. We all want to help one another, human beings are like that' (Chaplin, 1940). In response to Nazi militarism, which he associates with the prof-iteering of industrialized society, Chaplin asserts the redemptive qualities of nature and instinct, together with an idealization of the power of human empathy:

> Greed has poisoned men's souls, has barricaded the world with hate, has goose-stepped us into misery and bloodshed. We have developed speed but we have shut ourselves in. Machinery that gives us abundance has left us in want. Our knowledge has made us cynical, our cleverness hard and unkind. We think too much and feel too little. More than machinery we need humanity. More than cleverness we need kindness and gentleness. Without these qualities, life will be violent and all will be lost.
>
> (Chaplin, 1940)

As Alan Dale writes, 'the Barber embodies a concept of insignificance Chaplin associates with all kinds of worthiness – honesty, hard work, courtesy, gallantry, the whole load' (Dale, 2000: 47). In the concept of a society that can be saved by simplicity and considerateness, the Jewish Barber's speech demonstrates a clear continuity between Chaplin's cri-tique of dehumanizing labour in *Modern Times*, and what he perceived as the automatism of Hitler's fascism, 'unnatural men, machine men, with machine minds and machine hearts' (Chaplin, 1940). Chaplin has abandoned the structure of comedy and the business of slapstick by this point of the film, as historical circumstances do not allow for a traditional resolution. However, the implicit optimism of comedy strongly influences the finale, as the Jewish Barber's speech is superimposed over images of dignified Jewish families in pastoral exile. As sheaves of corn blow in the wind with the promise of a new tomorrow, Chaplin's political naivety seems terribly exposed. These images were utterly hollow for Theodor Adorno and Max Horkheimer who, in their 1944 essay 'The Culture Industry', felt they gave 'the lie to the anti-fascist plea for freedom' and served 'to confirm the immutability of circumstances' rather than proposing a radically new direction (Adorno and Horkheimer, 2001: 148–149). This would not be the last time anyone accused Chaplin of inchoate sentimentalism.

Becker's *Jakob the Liar* was the first important fictional narrative of the Jewish wartime experience to come from East Germany (the German Democratic Republic). The film tells the story of the middle-aged Jakob, living in the ghetto and forced to work in the freight yard. One night he is sent to the police station where he accidentally overhears a radio report of the Russian army's advance. Given hope by this news, he tells his friend Kowalski who pressures him to know how he could possibly have heard a radio in the ghetto. Jakob tells him the truth, but Kowalski refuses to believe he would have left the police station alive. Instead, Jakob tells them he has a radio hidden in his house. Soon, the entire ghetto is coming to him for news, and the more he prevaricates, the more convinced they become that he has access to forbidden information (a perfect example of Bergson's 'reciprocal interference of series'). Faced with the choice of either giving his neighbours hope or telling them the truth, Jakob chooses the former. In this, and Jakob's simulation of radio broadcasts to tell his niece fairy tales, we are asked to condone his fiction as a gift that momentarily relieves suffering by extending the promise of a happy ending. There is no happy ending, of course, and the final scene contrasts the journey to the concentration camp with a fairy tale projected onto the clouds, unhappily indicating the optimism and intangibility of fiction. For Sander L. Gilman, *Jakob the Liar* is one of the few successful humorous treatments of Holocaust material, because its comic aspects are expressions of the accidental rather than the precursors of absorption into a comic resolution. 'Accident', he writes, is the wellspring of comedy and laughter, not because it is the opposite of tragedy but because it is the instantiation of the random in life, over which one can only laugh or weep. Becker provides the ability to do both in *Jakob the Liar* and made it possible to use the elicitation of laughter as a means of presenting the unpresentable, not only in the Shoah, but the randomness of life.

(Gilman, 2000: 304)

Gilman's view of Benigni's film is quite different. *Life is Beautiful* ends with the liberation of the camps by the US army, and Joshua, the little boy who has been saved from brutality by his father's protective fiction, is hauled up onto a tank by a friendly soldier, just as his father predicted. In the concluding *deus ex machina* that also enables Joshua to be reunited with his mother, Gilman accuses Benigni of reducing the topic to fit the demands of form, as 'Benigni's promise is that there are no accidents, that at the end of the comedy the gods in the machine will arrive to resolve the action and rescue those in danger' (Gilman, 2000: 304). In the ultimate imposition of comic form, the imperative to fascist inhumanity is overridden: 'Benigni's laughter is proof that whatever else will happen the promise of the film, the rescue of the child, must take place. Our expectations are fulfilled, and we feel good about our laughter' (Gilman, 2000: 304).

The three Oscars and huge box office success of *Life is Beautiful* made it the biggest Italian film in history, and it has probably been seen by tens of millions of people since its release in 1998 (Ezrahi, 2001: 292). For its supporters, Benigni has produced an important recognition of Italy's participation in the deportation of Jews, and told a fable of selfless love and the ability of the spirit to resist the most appalling oppression. The worst accusations levelled at it insist that it is sanitized, fabricated, dishonest, and 'a whitewash of European guilt' (Ezrahi, 2001: 295). In his review of the film published in the November 1998 issue of *Time* magazine, Richard Shickel argued that the comic framework of the film amounted to an insult to the actual witnesses of the Holocaust, writing that 'its living victims . . . inevitably grow fewer each year. The voices that would deny it ever took place remain strident. In this climate, turning even a small corner of this century's central horror into feel-good entertainment is abhorrent. Sentimentality is a kind of fascism too' (quoted in

Flanzbaum, 2001: 281). A similar degree of outrage was expressed by David Denby in The *New Yorker*, who accused Benigni of wanting 'the authority of the Holocaust without the actuality' and of 'feeling relieved and happy that *Life is Beautiful* is a benign form of Holocaust denial' (quoted in Flanzbaum, 2001: 282). It is easy to see comic structure as a primary cause of this distaste, coupled with the fact that it was devised and performed by a non-Jewish comedian, making the film open to accusations of careless optimism and inauthenticity. Rather than seeking to define some truth of the Holocaust and Italy's part in it, the film provides only easy comic solutions and belief in a Christianized conception of abso-lution, 'the comic as artificial human construct of the universe *as it should be*' (Ezrahi, 2001: 307). Ruth Ben-Ghiat argues that Benigni's film also tries to deflect some of the attention away from the Holocaust as a specifically Jewish tragedy through 'the inclusion of a self-sacrificing Christian wife [who] affirms that Jews have no monopoly in Italy on the state of victimhood, even as they remain the most acceptable public symbols of fascism's inhumanity' (Ben-Ghiat, 2001: 263). In response to these criticisms, however, several writers have argued that the way in which Holocaust history has come to be policed results in any treatment of it being instantly condemned as facile, with the effect that a number of valid narratives are dismissed out of hand. Hilene Flanzbaum, for example, points to a contradiction amongst those who reject Benigni's film, because they occupy 'a paradoxical and infinite regress in which critics feel obliged to repeat that the Holocaust cannot ever be truly represented, while at the same time, these very same critics vigorously complain each time an individual representation insufficiently portrays the event' (Flanzbaum, 2001: 284). For her, *Life Is Beautiful* 'acknowledges at the start that it is a myth, and in so doing, it clearly – and I believe, more honestly than films that claim historical veracity – accepts its limitations as a work of art' (Flanzbaum, 2001: 283). As long as we understand that the film is a fictional construct, Benigni's treatment is justified exactly because it does not claim to be an authentic history, but does other work by placing the issues in an entirely new and unusual context that has the virtue of reach-ing an enormous audience. While not satisfied that the film is entirely innocent of all the accusations levelled at it, Flanzbaum concludes that, 'Benigni accomplishes a great deal when he defamiliarizes the Holocaust enough to make such viewers feel it all over again' (Flanzbaum, 2001: 283).

Perhaps the question of comedy and politics might be reduced to questions of this kind, questions of efficacy. When laughter is directed aggressively, it can be an extremely powerful tool, victimizing its targets in purely negative terms and reinforcing prejudice. Comedy that seeks to do the same to tyrannical or prejudicial ideologies, however, often has to relinquish a reasonable base for its arguments before it enters the arena. Parody and satire are good for demolishing dogma but not for constructively offering alternatives to it. Alternative comedy found itself censoring guilty form to the extent that it struggled to find material and had to replace blacks and women with red-haired people and Margaret Thatcher. Holocaust comedies exist within such a complicated terrain of history, representation, politics, and prejudice that they become instantly suspect, with the result that both comedy and politics lose their immediacy and productions become debatable at best and ineffective and insulting at worst. Perhaps it is true that comedy has nothing to offer politics when the project requires something more than simple derision. Maybe the limited usefulness of comedy in politics is a function of laughter's association with ridicule. Let us then turn our attention to the question of laughter, what it is, and how it is used.

6

LAUGHTER

Perhaps even if nothing else today has any future, our *laughter* may yet have a future.

Friedrich Nietzsche

Satisfactory explanations of laughter have always been notoriously elusive. As Bergson put it, 'this little problem . . . has a knack of baffling every effort, of slipping away only to bob up again, a pert challenge flung at philosophical speculation' (Bergson, 1980: 61). Across the centuries, laughter has been variously understood as vice or cowardice, as delight caused by surprise, the product of defamiliarization, a means of averting antisocial conflict, or an extra-linguistic bark signalling the limits of understanding. Aristotle, noting that laughter is exclusive to human beings, believed that an infant could not be considered truly human until it had laughed its first laugh at forty days old. By acknowledging laughter as essentially human, every discussion of it also tends to contain an idea of what being human means. A further phenomenon unifies all theories of laughter: they all take it to be the manifestation of a perfectly serious urge, process, or function, just like Dutch historian Johann Huizinga's theory of the serious importance of play. Laughter is never just fun, as in all accounts of it the human being is using their laughter to serve a social, psychological, or physiological need. This chapter will survey a number of the most prominent theories of laughter in order to show how this idea, so closely associated with comedy, has been used as a means of understanding human identity.

CHRISTIAN LAUGHTER

Early Christianity was hostile to laughter. Nowhere does the New Testament mention Christ laughing, although he twice wept, and evidence for his sense of humour is scant. The early church equated levity and mirth with foolishness and ignorance. Ecclesiastes states that,

> The heart of the wise is in the house of mourning; but the heart of fools is in the house of mirth. It is better to hear the rebuke of the wise, than for a man to hear the song of fools. For as the crackling of thorns under a pot, so is the laughter of the fool: this also is vanity.
>
> (Ecclesiastes 7: 4–6)

Early Christian converts in Rome founded their principles of conduct in opposition to the luxurious and debauched lives of their pagan masters. Christian theology actively rewarded simplicity and poverty, and found virtue in privation and self-control. The abrogation of the body and the rigid imposition of pious abstinence made physical pleasure suspicious. In Philippa Pullar's words, 'the body *had* to be broken; it had to be abused and maltreated, its reactions, sensations and natural functions became to the Christians a real and terrible neurosis' (Pullar, 2001: 37). The contrast between Roman and Christian attitudes to laughter is apparent in the story of St Genesius, a pagan Roman actor and now the patron saint of comedians. During a performance for the Emperor Diocletian that parodied the Christian baptism, Genesius received an angelic visitation that delivered an admonition. His laughter quickly turned to mortification and servility as he asked forgiveness of his newly discovered God. Diocletian, who was expecting a laugh, had him stretched, beheaded, and burnt (Jacobson, 1997: 163–164). Laughter, then, was a vulgar eruption of the body that contained the indecent excess of paganism and was impudent, raucous, and ill-disciplined: 'Sorrow is better than laughter: for by the sadness of the countenance the heart is made better' (Ecclesiastes 7: 3).

As we saw in Chapter 4, governing the body requires the regulation and the repression of certain corporeal traits. In early Christianity, it was conventional to understand the human subject as fundamentally torn between the animalistic urges of the flesh and the sanctity of a pious soul. The earliest ascetic condemnation of laughter, authored in the second century by Clement of Alexandria, conceded that laughter was human, but urged Christians to restrain it as they might similar bestial instincts:

> For, in a word, whatever things are natural to men we must not eradicate from them, but rather impose on them limits and suitable times. For man is not to laugh on all occasions because he is a laughing animal, any more than the horse neighs on all occasions because he is a neighing animal. But as rational beings, we are to regulate ourselves suitably, harmoniously relaxing the austerity and over-tension of our serious pursuits, not inharmoniously breaking them up altogether.
>
> (Clement of Alexandria, 1983: 250)

In the process of determining pious deportment, laughter became subject to the rules of appropriate behaviour and the rational ordinances of self-control that kept base instincts in check. Clement was particularly wary of the susceptibility of women to laughter, equating their mirth with sexual immorality: 'the discordant relaxation of countenance in the case of women is called a giggle, and is meretricious laughter' (Clement of Alexandria, 1983: 250). Ascetic control of the body was clearly troubled by occasions that might convulse, distort, and overthrow it, and in women the repercussions might be damnable. Similarly, early monastic life held laughing to be one of its greatest crimes. As Jerry Palmer writes:

> In the earliest monastic regulations (in the fifth century) laughter is condemned as the grossest breach of the rule of silence, and later it is considered a breach of the rule of humility; it is also considered the greatest dirtying of the mouth, which should be a filter for good and evil to enter and leave the body; therefore it must be prevented.
>
> (Palmer, 1994: 44)

Both examples, of female reserve and monastic silence, are indicative of the belief that 'the more the body was closed against the world, the more the soul was opened up to God' (Gilhus, 1997: 67).

While the early church made significant attempts to banish and condemn laughter, the medieval period saw ecclesiastical authorities drawing it into the liturgical calendar and distinguishing between good laughter and bad. The enigmatic question of whether or not Jesus had laughed in his early life enjoyed a vogue in ecclesiastical society, so much that in the thirteenth century, the University of Paris organized an annual conference on the subject (Le Goff, 1997: 43). In Chapter 2, we saw how medieval culture made the figure of folly into a universal symbol of human ignorance. Similarly in medieval morality plays the role of Vice was given to a clown to better underline the need for folly to be overcome before Mankind can proceed to Grace. 'If there were no devils to expel, there would be no comedy to enjoy', writes Howard Jacobson, adding that, during the medieval period 'hell remained a locus for hilarity' (Jacobson, 1997: 151). Stage Hell mouths would repeatedly provide the entrance for the most amusing comic entertainers. A remnant of this practice can be seen in the devils chasing clowns in Christopher Marlowe's *Doctor Faustus* (1594). Jacobson also lists a number of *Ioculatores Domini*, jokers and jesters of God, canonized holy men, including St Francis of Assisi, who used humour in their proselytizing (Jacobson, 1997: 166). Religious festivals, such as the Feast of Fools, are further examples of the reconciliation of laughter with religion. While Pope Innocent III (1198–1216) issued a decree condemning the Feast of Fools, in pragmatic terms the incorporation of laughter into worship was a necessity if the church were to extend its authority over areas of folk belief and folk practices, including the still-thriving Roman Saturnalia that it had so far failed to assimilate. The moral equation of laughter with vice remained, but it was now utilized in ritual as an instructive counterpoint to official discourse that emphasized human failings and therefore the necessity of spiritual intervention. In rituals of this kind, laughter serves joyfully to instruct humility and the distance between the human and the divine. Laughter in the Middle Ages therefore expressed human folly and postlapsarian weakness, a liturgically important rite of exorcism. Enid Welsford argues that the Feast of the Fools should not be thought of as a decline into idiocy, so much as a demonstration of a subtle intelligence that understood the antagonisms between riot and ritual as fundamental aspects of human existence (Welsford, 1935: 202). Medieval laughter was part of creation, it had an exegetical purpose that could find the truth of the gospel in the pious and the grotesque, rather than through a rigid, contrasting system of truth and its opposite.

In addition to the metaphysical implications of laughter, there was a tradition in early modern medicine that stressed its healthful benefits. Influenced by Hippocrates (*c*.460–357 BC), the most celebrated physician of antiquity, and Democritus (b. *c*.460 BC), the 'laughing philosopher', both of whom had encouraged the cultivation of a sense of humour as a defence against illness and depression, medical men such as Laurent Joubert (1529–82) and, of course, Rabelais, saw laughter as a means of maintaining the body's humoral balance. Joubert, whose *Treatise on Laughter* (1560) presents itself as a scientific investigation, writes that 'being joyful and ready to laugh indicates a good nature and purity of blood, [and] thus contributes to the health of the body and the mind' (Joubert, 1980: 126). After recounting three detailed stories about the laughter-provoking actions of monkeys at the bedside of the dangerously ill, he concludes that 'the dignity and excellence of laughter is . . . very great inasmuch as it reinforces the spirit so much that it can suddenly change the state of the patient, and from his deathbed render him curable' (Joubert, 1980: 128).

Bakhtin, apparently inspired by the restorative function attributed to laughter by early modern science, extends its implications into the political arena by crediting it with the ability to triumph over oppression: 'festive folk laughter presents an element of victory not only over super-natural awe, of the sacred over death; it also means the defeat of power, of earthly kings, of the earthly upper classes, of all that oppresses and restricts' (Bakhtin, 1984: 92). Largely silenced by an official culture that consolidates its power through seriousness, Bakhtin's laughter is the popular voice of the people, not only alleviating the tensions of official ideology, but cutting right through them and denying their influence. As we shall see shortly, this conception of laughter as an extra-linguistic challenge to systems of order is a notion that enjoys some popularity in twentieth-century criticism.

SUPERIORITY AND INCONGRUITY THEORIES

The superiority theory of laughter states that human beings are moved to laugh when presented with a person or situation they feel themselves to be intellectually, morally, or physically above. Bakhtin's argument claims that by the sixteenth century a reorganization of intellectual categories under the auspices of humanism continued to separate laughter from official culture. This led to a starker demarcation of the serious and the comic where 'that which is important and essential cannot be comical', and 'the essential truth about the world and man cannot be told in the language of laughter' (Bakhtin, 1984: 67). Laughter was removed from its position in philosophy and turned into scorn, becoming 'a light amusement or a form of salutary social punishment of corrupt and low persons' (Bakhtin, 1984: 67). We can certainly see that the concept of laughter changes in the sixteenth and seventeenth centuries, in a way that imbues it with an ethical significance. Sir Philip Sidney, for example, remarked that laughter 'hath only a scornful tickling' (Sidney, 1991: 68). This attitude is developed further in studies of rhetoric in the period. Thomas Wilson's *The Arte of Rhetoricke* (1567) provides a perfect example of the humanist conception of laughter. 'The occasion of laughter', he writes,

> and the meane that maketh us merrie . . . is the fondnes, the filthiness, the deformitie, and al suche evil behaviour, as we se to bee in each other. For we laugh always at those thinges, which either onely, or chiefly touche handsomely, and wittely, some speciall fault, or fond behavior in some one body or some one thing.
>
> (Wilson, 1567: f.69, verso)

Laughter is used in rhetoric as a means of besting one's opponent. This idea is borrowed directly from Cicero (103–43 BC), the father and codifier of oratorical arts and hero of the humanists, who writes:

> It clearly becomes an orator to raise laughter . . . merriment naturally wins goodwill for its author; and everyone admires acuteness, which is often concentrated in a single word, uttered generally in repelling, though sometimes in delivering, an attack; and it shatters or obstructs or makes light of an opponent, or alarms or repulses him; and it shows the orator himself to be a man of finish, accomplishment and taste.
>
> (Cicero, 1984: 28)

Fritz Gaf writes that Roman laughter was mainly intended to 'to correct deviance – in a socially acceptable way' (Gaf, 1997: 31). The importance of rhetoric in humanism may therefore have had the effect of replacing medieval conceptions of redemptive, inclusive laughter with the idea of it as a weapon used in verbal conflict and directed specifically against failure or weaknesses. Thinking of laughter as a weapon would therefore allow us to think of it as an ethically determined tool, one that can be applied to both good and bad ends. Certainly mockery and ridicule in Tudor and Stuart England were prevalent means of extending social norms. Michael Bristol tells us that

> ridicule is a recognized element in law enforcement, in the punishment of insubordination and in the everyday feeling of superiority enjoyed by nobles in respect to their servants. Laughter is also an important element in the strategies of social appeasement used by servants in respect of their masters. Self-abjection and self-ridicule are significant elements in an elaborate system of deferential gesture and compliment.
>
> (Bristol, 1985: 126)

From this idea, it is not far to 'superiority theory', one of the three most durable explanations of laughter in Western culture. By far the most famous representative of superiority theory is the seventeenth-century English philosopher Thomas Hobbes. In truth, Hobbes had little to say about laughter, but what he did say is quoted in almost every discussion of the subject, even though his ambiguity towards the topic is clear when he calls laughter the signal of a 'passion that hath no name' (Hobbes, 1840: 45). 'Laughter', he wrote in his *Human Nature* (1650), 'is nothing else but a sudden glory arising from some sudden conception of some eminency in ourselves, by comparison with the infirmity of others, or with our own formerly' (Hobbes, 1840: 46). For Hobbes, laughter is always antagonistic and conflictual, establishing a hierarchy at the moment of pleasure. In *Leviathan* (1660), he makes his ethical objection to this clear when he states that 'much laughter at the defects of others is a sign of Pusillanimity' (Hobbes, 1991: 43). Even laughter that is not immediately directed at an 'inferior' person actually present is structured according to this principle: 'Laughter without offense, must be at absurdities and infirmities abstracted from persons, and when all the company may laugh together' (Hobbes, 1840: 46–47). Clearly, there are types of humour that depend on a feeling of superiority for their operation. Racist and sexist jokes, for example, presume an ethnic, gendered, and intellectual advantage on the part of the teller and his audience. Yet it is also possible to see that much laughter does not arise from a feeling of pre-eminence, even one that is suppressed or inverted. Like the early Christian commentators, Hobbes's definition belongs to the tradition that understands laughter operating within a moral framework that sees laughers as self-regarding and uncharitable. Superiority theory even became an edict of manners in eighteenth-century 'men of quality' who refused to laugh on grounds of breeding. In one of his comprehensive letters, Lord Chesterfield (1694–1773) warns his son that he should be,

> never heard to laugh while you live. Frequent and loud laughter is the characteristic of folly and ill manners. . . . In my mind nothing so illiberal, and so ill-bred as audible laughter . . . how low and unbecoming a thing laughter is. Not to mention the disagreeable noise it makes, and the shocking distortion of the face it occasions.
>
> (Stanhope, 1929: 49)

Here we find the Christian disapprobation of laughter and its fear of bodily disorder, yet both are overridden by a class consciousness that sees laughter as the enemy of social distinctions. According to Samuel Johnson, neither Swift nor Pope could be induced to laugh, and Lord Froth in Congreve's *The Double Dealer* (1694) states, 'There is nothing more unbecoming a Man of Quality than to laugh; Jesu, 'tis such a vulgar expression of the passion! Everybody can laugh' (Congreve, 1973: 7). The class-based rejection of laughter penetrated further than the fear of appearing vulgar. Addison claimed that laughter 'slackens and unbraces the Mind, weakens the Faculties, and causes a Kind of Remissness, and Dissolution in all the powers of the soul' (Addison and Steele, 1979, vol. 2: 237–238). That every important household used to keep a jester is conclusive proof that 'everyone diverts himself with some person or other that is below him in Point of Understanding, and triumphs in the Superiority of his Genius, whilst he has such objects of derision in his eyes' (Addison and Steele, 1979, vol. 1: 142–143). Superiority theory was therefore confirmed by the superior members of society refraining from laughing.

The continuity of superiority theory, and a general disdain for laughter in elite circles, was eventually challenged in the eighteenth century by analyses of humour that indicated the importance of pleasure in laughter over mockery and derision. Superiority theory operates in the absence of a joke and focuses on physical defects, personal misfortunes, and social inequality; as such its view of humour is dictated by grotesque and burlesque forms. The new accent of eighteenth-century laughter studies highlighted the linguistic formulae of humour, the operation of verbal triggers, and the juxtaposition of elements in the production of comic effects. Francis Hutcheson (1694–1746), professor of Philosophy at the University of Glasgow, was an early and effective challenger to the Hobbesian position. Writing in The *Dublin Journal* in 1726, Hutcheson attacked the malevolent theory of laughter remarking that when we laugh there is a 'great fund of pleasantry' (Hutcheson, 1750: 7). Hutcheson was keen to prove that laughter and a sense of the ridiculous 'is plainly of considerable moment in human society' and 'is exceeding useful to abate our concerns or resentment' in matters of small affront or inappropriate conduct (Hutcheson, 1750: 32). Indeed, he found 'that nature has given us a sense of the ridiculous as an avenue to pleasure and a remedy for sorrow' (Trave, 1960: 69). A new generation of writers began to praise the corrective, admonitory aspects of comedy over its corrosive qualities. Shaftesbury's *Sensus Communis* finds humour a 'lenitive Remedy against Vice, and a kind of Specifick against Superstition and Melancholy Delusion' (Shaftesbury, 1988: 188). In addition, Hutcheson makes the elegant point that if laughter were only prompted by a feeling of pre-eminence, then it would surely be easier to elicit. 'Strange!', he writes, 'that none of the Hobbists banish canary birds and squirrels, and lap-dogs and pugs, and cats out of their houses, and substitute in their places asses, and owls, and snails, and oysters to be merry upon' (Hutcheson, 1750: 12). In other words, if a person can be moved to laughter by confirmation of his or her superiority, then any time they felt like laughing they need only look upon the animals.

The idea that most clearly represents a rejection of superiority theory is Hutcheson's belief that the risible emanated from a juxtaposition of incompatible contrasts. By the means of a discussion of great men on the toilet he explains that the ludicrous is generated by the combination of high and low in a single scene: 'the jest is increased by the dignity, gravity, or modesty of the person,' he writes, 'which shows that it is this contrast, or opposition of ideas and dignity and meanness, which is the occasion of laughter' (Hutcheson, 1750: 21). In the image of the great man otherwise occupied, greatness and gravity collide with lowering bodily urgency. Henry Fielding makes a similar point in his preface to the novel *Joseph Andrews* (1742). The unfortunate, deformed, or disproportionate are not humorous in themselves, he writes, but may become so if they adopt an affectation:

> Surely he hath a very ill-framed Mind, who can look on Ugliness, Infirmity, or Poverty, as ridiculous in themselves: nor do I believe any Man living who meets a dirty Fellow riding through the Streets in a Cart, is struck with an Idea of the Ridiculous from it; but if he should see the same Figure descend from his Coach and Six, or bolt from his Chair with his Hat under his Arm, he would then begin to laugh, and with justice.

> (Fielding, 1980: 7)

Pursuing the clash of incompatible ideas, James Beattie (1735–1803), professor of Moral Philosophy and Logic at the University of Aberdeen, writes in his essay 'On Laughter and Ludicrous Composition':

> Laughter arises from the view of two or more inconsistent, unsuitable, or incongruous parts or circumstances, considered as united in one complex object or assemblage, or as acquiring a sort of mutual relation from the peculiar manner in which the mind takes notice of them.

> (Beattie, 1776: 347)

While Beattie was not the first to use the words 'incongruous' or 'incongruity' in relation to humour (that honour belongs to Mark Akenside's *Pleasures of Imagination* (1744)), his definition of laughter's trigger is entirely representative of the shift in dominance from superiority to incongruity theories in the eighteenth century, and is the key to humour upheld by philosophers such as Kant and Schopenhauer. The new focus on incongruity appears to be historically appropriate to the eighteenth century where aleatory wit and linguistic invention were culturally privileged skills. Addison, who while disapproving of laughter celebrated wit, gives an account of the latter as follows,

> That every resemblance of Ideas is not that which we call Wit, unless it be such an one that gives *Delight* and *Surprize* to the Reader: These two Properties seem essential to Wit, more particularly the last of them. In order therefore that the Resemblance in the Ideas be Wit, it is necessary that the Ideas should not lie too near one another in the Nature of things; for where the Likeness is obvious, it gives no Surprize.
>
> (Addison and Steele, 1979, vol. 1: 189)

What is apparent in this description is the similarity between Addison's definition and Hutcheson's and Beattie's discussions of laughter's triggers. Wit, according to Addison, resides in the inventive drawing together of apparently distant ideas for the amusement and intellectual thrill of the listener. Again, we see the importance of crossing ideational boundaries and the bringing of one thing into a taxonomy to which it is not considered to belong. As incongruity plays with taxonomies and hierarchies it suggests that these hierarchies are permeable and fluid rather than rigid and permanent. The collision or juxtaposition of the great with the low, or the humble adopting the airs of the elite, take their humour from a displacement of order that simultaneously acknowledges order and reveals its absurdity. Pleasure in wit also does this, as it recognizes the role of chance in the production of meaning, and the ability of language to make meanings outside the realm of practical sense. However, critics of incongruity theory point out that it over-privileges structural aspects in the production of laughter as if the formula of juxtaposition alone were the trigger. As John Lippitt writes, 'even if, in any given example of humour, it is possible to identify an element of incongruity, it is not necessarily this incongruity itself which is the predominant reason for amusement. To put all the emphasis on a factor such as incongruity is to stress form or structure at the expense of content' (Lippitt, 1992: 200). Presumably, then, there has to be a reason why some things are funny and others are not, which leads us on to explanations rooted in culture and the unconscious.

RELIEF THEORY: FREUD AND SPENCER

The successor to incongruity theory was in some respects a continued and internalized version of it. Nineteenth- and early twentieth-century considerations of laughter, particularly those of Herbert Spencer and Sigmund Freud, saw the triggers of laughter not so much as a recognition of incongruity within scenarios or linguistic formulae, but as a symptom of division and struggle within the self, recognition, as it were, of incongruous selfhood. This is known as 'release' or 'relief' theory. The impact of Freud's 'discovery' of the unconscious is clearly of great relevance to an understanding of the process that recognizes conflicted impulses within subjectivity as a cause of laughter. From this principle, Freud theorized that humour works because it appeals to unconscious thoughts that remain largely hidden in the majority of our social interactions. This would explain the concept of a relative and individuated 'sense of humour' not shared by all, as individual psyches are wont to find different topics or ideas humorously appealing based on the different experiences that have helped to shape them.

The mechanics of Freud's theory of laughter are not entirely his, but rather based in part on the work of Herbert Spencer (1820–1903), the father of evolutionary philosophy. Spencer attributed laughter to a physiological cause, proposing the flow of 'nerve force', internal energy that is generated by cerebral activity and which circulates in the body until it is discharged by muscular action, such as conversation, or respiration. On occasion, nervous energy will be displaced from its proper outlet and redirect itself in short bursts of activity such as heavy breathing, jumping up and down, or rubbing one's hands with glee. Laughter, like released steam pressure, is a manifestation of the internal redirection of nervous energy. This was not an entirely new idea. The anonymous author of *An Essay on Laughter* (1769) describes the physiological effect as a '*laughter-struggle*' (Anon., 1769: 75), an internal battle between the mind and the muscles. Spencer holds that 'laughter naturally results when consciousness is unawares transferred from great things to small', when an anticipated sequence of thoughts is bathetically interrupted with the result that the accumulated nervous energy of one emotion now needs to be to be re-channelled and provided with an alternative outlet (Spencer, 1860: 400). Spencer imagines internal channels along which nervous energy flows. The grander or more serious the emotion, the more the channels dilate. If a sequence of ideas were to then take a ludicrous turn, the channels become restricted and the surplus of energy expends itself: 'the excess must therefore discharge itself in some other direction; and . . . there results an efflux through the motor nerves to various classes of the muscles, producing the half convulsive actions we call laughter' (Spencer, 1860: 400). Laughter, then, is always the product of a lowering of anticipated ideas, although these can have healthful effects: 'The heart and stomach must come in for a fair share of discharge', he adds, 'And thus there seems to be a good physiological basis for the popular notion that laughter facilitates the digestion' (Spencer, 1860: 401).

While Spencer's hydraulic explanation of laughter may not have aged well, it is worth considering for its influence on Freud's analysis of the question in his 1905 study, *Jokes and Their Relation to the Unconscious*. Freud's theory is in general agreement with Spencer's model of laughter as redirected internal energy, although he modifies it beyond a biological explanation and explains the need for energetic redirection as the circumvention of internal prohibitions put in place by the superego. Jokes in Freud can be used as a means of making public statements about taboo topics: 'a purpose being satisfied whose satisfaction would otherwise not have taken place' (Freud, 2001: 117). Freud's discussion of laughter occurs within the context of laughter as a response to jokes only, and two types of joke in particular that he identifies as 'innocent' and 'tendentious'. The innocent joke is essentially a pun or word game and appeals because of its technique and formal qualities, its play on words or transposition of concepts, as in Freud's example: 'Not only did he not believe in ghosts; he wasn't even frightened of them' (Freud, 2001: 92). As for the tendentious joke, says Freud, 'there are only two purposes that it may serve, and these two can themselves be subsumed under a single heading. It is either a *hostile* joke (serving the purpose of aggressiveness, satire, or defence), or an *obscene* joke (serving the purpose of exposure)' (Freud, 2001: 97). The need for these jokes is a response to social expectations, as the norms of etiquette usually prevent us from directly insulting others or broaching taboo subjects. By touching on these difficult topics, the joke does important work, as it alleviates the inhibition of the joker and addresses the taboo while also keeping it in place. Laughing is the audible signal that the energy required for 'cathexis', the accumulation of energy around an idea, has been lifted and can now be dispersed in a pleasurable fashion. The joker, says Freud,

> has saved his psychological expenditure. . . . We should say that his pleasure corresponds to this economy. Our insight into the mechanism of laughter leads us rather to the introduction of the proscribed idea by means of an auditory perception, the cathectic energy used for the inhibition has now suddenly become superfluous and has been lifted, and is therefore now ready to be discharged by laughter.
>
> (Freud, 2001: 148–149)

Laughter, then, is the bang of anti-social thoughts colliding with a censorious brick wall: 'in laughter', writes Freud, 'the conditions are present under which a sum of psychical energy which has hitherto been used for cathexis is allowed discharge' (Freud, 2001: 148). Like Spencer, Freud's concept of laughter fits into an internal economy, a functional system that retains the equilibrium of the subject by disposing of waste in a socially acceptable way, and so maintaining mental health.

POSTSTRUCTURALIST LAUGHTERS

Milan Kundera's novel, *The Book of Laughter and Forgetting* (1980), contains a scene in which two students, wearing cardboard horns, and their teacher begin to giggle uncontrollably during a class discussion of Eugene Ionesco's play *Rhinoceros*:

> The three women danced and laughed, the cardboard noses juggled, and the class looked at them in mute horror. But by now the three dancing women were unaware of the others, they were concentrating entirely on themselves and on their sensual pleasure. Suddenly Madame Raphael stamped her foot harder and rose a few centimetres above the floor and then, with the next step, was no longer touching the ground. She pulled her two companions after her, and in a moment all three were revolving above the floor and rising slowly in a spiral. When their hair touched the ceiling, it started little by little to open. They rose higher and higher through that opening, their cardboard noses were no longer visible, and now there were only three pairs of shoes passing through

the gaping hole, but these too finally vanished, while from on high, the dumbfounded students heard the fading, radiant laughter of the three archangels.

(Kundera, 1996: 104)

Kundera's novel, set predominantly in communist Czechoslovakia, deals with personal relationships and asks if anything can remain private in an intrusive system. Weighed down by alienation and misunderstandings, laughter is the sound that accompanies freedom, a fantasy of weightlessness and unobstructed movement. This is laughter as an expression of the sublime: joyful, angelic, desperate, exhausted, overwhelmed, substituting for speech when nothing can possibly be said. This small scene in some ways represents the manner in which laughter has been conceived in the variety of arguments grouped together under the term poststructuralism in the twentieth century. This is not to say that postructuralism has adopted Kundera's depiction of a radiant laughter that transports one to a paradise far from the reach of oppressive law, but it has configured laughter as a trope that expresses a sense of the beyond, of something outside language and cognition as it is organized in the quotidian. Following a theme established in the work of Friedrich Nietzsche, what Simon Critchley has called 'the golden laughter of tragic affirmation' (Critchley, 2002: 105), poststructuralist laughter acts like a sonar, reaching out and signalling the limit of everything that can be said and understood. This laughter is not an expression of pleasure, superiority, or release; nor is it nonsense, the worthless opposite of intelligibility. Rather, laughter acts as a powerful recognition of the end of understanding in language and the comic recognition of the subject's failure to grasp it. Georges Bataille has written of laughter as 'that place where nothing counts any-more – neither the "object", nor the "subject"' (quoted in Borch-Jacobsen, 1987: 741). Following Bataille closely, Mikkel Borch-Jacobsen speaks of laughter as the end of identity and absolute finitude: 'it is the *presentation*, necessarily pathetic and miniscule, of NOTHING . . . NOTHING is the impossible, the impossible to present, and thus its presentation can be nothing other than a comedy, risible and ridiculous' (Borch-Jacobsen, 1987: 756). While not entirely unlike Bakhtin's soaring laughter of liberation, this formulation of laughter neither rejuvenates nor serves as a palliative against oppressive seriousness. This is not laughter as a release from oppression, but laughter that encounters the limits of all conceptual formulae and returns to acknowledge the finitude of its own existence. Critchley offers this useful explanation,

> Laughter is an acknowledgement of finitude, precisely not a manic affirmation of finitude in the solitary, neurotic laughter of the mountain tops (all too present in imitators of Nietzsche, although administered with liberal doses of irony by Nietzsche himself), but as an affirmation that finitude cannot be affirmed because it cannot be grasped. . . . Laughter returns us to that limited condition of our finitude, the shabby and degenerating state of our upper and lower bodily strata, and it is here that the comic allows the windows to fly open onto our tragic condition.
>
> (Critchley, 1997: 159)

What appears to be the intangible, impermanent, extra-linguistic nature of laughter has appealed to some writers on deconstruction. The self-reflexive structure of deconstructive readings, their interest in 'play', effective repetitions, aporia (the expression of doubt), and linguistic and etymological puns have been understood as an innovative and necessary incorporation of a type of laughter in work that engages with the foundational discourses of philosophy, discourses from which laughter has previously been excluded. Jean-Luc Nancy sees the utility of a concept of laughter to deconstruction: 'Laughter is neither a presence nor an absence, it is the giving of a presence in its own disappearance. Not given, but giving, and thus suspended on the edge of its own presentation . . . laughter is the giving of an infinite variety of possible faces and meanings. It is, in a word, the repetition of this offer' (Nancy, 1987: 729). Understood this way, laughter is a form of the Derridean concept of *différance*, a way of thinking of language as a structure of infinite referral and deferral, in which there are no fully meaningful terms, only traces of terms. In a piece that specifically focuses on the work of French philosopher of language Jacques Derrida (1930–), Nancy continues the thematization of laughter as a trope that can be used to interrogate the problem of the absent or deferred presence of full meaning that is a key theme in deconstructive work. Deconstruction argues that the centre or core of meaning, the plentiful 'originary' truth that validates all thought and understanding, whether it be envisaged as a theological or philosophical concept, can never be revealed through language but only ever be alluded to and infinitely deferred. For Nancy, this absent centre can be reconceived as a laugh. 'The origin is laughing', he writes, 'There is a transcendental laugh':

> What is a transcendental laugh? It is not the obverse of the sign or value accorded to serious matters, which thinking, necessarily, reclaims. It is knowledge of a condition of possibility which gives nothing to know. There is nothing comic about it: it is neither nonsense nor irony. This laugh does not laugh *at* anything. It laughs at nothing, for nothing. It signifies nothing, without ever being absurd. It laughs at being the peal of its laughter, we might say. Which is not to say that it is unserious or that it is painless. It is beyond all opposition of serious and non-serious, of pain and pleasure. Or rather, it is at the juncture of these oppositions, at the limit of which they share and which itself is only the limit of each one of these terms, the limit of their signification.
>
> (Nancy, 1992: 41)

Laughter comes to symbolize the absent origin that has no full significance of its own, but which is constitutive of conceptual attempts to positively structure systems of meaning. What is noteworthy in this formulation is the extraction of the comic from its understanding of laughter. Instead of thinking of laughter as the opposite of gravity and intellectual seriousness, Nancy asks it to represent a fundamental contradiction that affronts modes of understanding grounded in reason. As such, laughter is a kind of metaphysical contradiction encountered at the boundary of reason.

The French feminist critic Hélène Cixous offers us a similar image of laughter as sound of signification at the limits of signification. Her famous essay 'The Laugh of the Medusa', a title that evokes an idea of mythical female monstrosity and 'outsidedness', deals with the acts of definition that constitute the formulation of gender distinctions in language. Cixous calls for a redefinition of gender distinctions through a revolution in signification, a redeployment of language capable of countering the domination of language by patriarchy, a language that can 'break up the "truth" with laughter' (Cixous, 1976: 888). The laugh of the Medusa is the revolutionary call of the woman outside patriarchal definitions; this laughter rejects phallocentric identification, and is forging a new language:

> Too bad for them if they fall apart upon discovering that women aren't men, or that the mother doesn't have one. But isn't this fear convenient for them? Wouldn't the worst be, isn't the worst, in truth, that women aren't castrated, that they only have to stop listening to the Sirens (for the Sirens were men) for history to change its meaning? You only have to look at the Medusa straight on to see her. And she's not deadly. She's beautiful, and she's laughing.
>
> (Cixous, 1976: 855)

As Frances Gray has written, 'for Cixous, the laughter of the Medusa destroys all hierarchies by rendering nonsensical the aggression between father and son that is their basis; in destroying hierarchy it will remove all difference between margin and centre. Women will not be outsiders, because the concept of the "outside" or "inside" will become meaningless' (Gray, 1994: 37). This is laughter as a radical commentary that refuses to work inside the significatory system established by the oppressor, busy about the work of dismantling patriarchal structures of knowledge.

The Marxist critics Theodor Adorno and Max Horkheimer, writing in 1944, held a radically different view of the uses of laughter. For them, 'Fun is a medicinal bath' (Adorno and Horkheimer, 2001: 140). While poststructuralism treats laughter as a trope with some allegorical significance, Adorno and Horkheimer see it only as an empty reminder of a previously satisfying experience. The 'culture industry', they argue, referring to mainstream art and media under capitalism, manipulates laughter and uses it as a placebo which it feeds to the population of the 'false society' through television and film in order to divert them from reflecting on their inauthentic existence. The culture industry's mass-market debasement of art, they argue, reduces content to prudish titillation, and, having dispensed with aesthetic challenges, mass-market culture resorts to humour as a means of obscuring the vacuity it peddles at the expense of critical thought. The laughter of the culture industry is therefore a kind of infantilized false consciousness, attached to images in films that allude to the gratification of desires, such as kissing or the possibility of sexual intercourse. By framing these scenes as risible, vicarious thrills, the culture industry substitutes genuine pleasure and experience for a humorous alternative so that 'jovial denial takes the place of the pain found in ecstasy and in asceticism' (Adorno and Horkheimer, 2001: 141).

Laughter is offered instead of satisfaction; it is a means of rendering all desires and ambition beyond those provided by capitalism as a ludicrous and stupid propositions, as 'The supreme law is that they shall not satisfy their desires at any price; they must laugh and be content with laughter' (Adorno and Horkheimer, 2001: 141). In conclusion we may say that poststructuralist and theoretical treatments of laughter have been attracted to its intangibility and association with a level of somatic existence beyond that mediated by language, an existence that therefore lends laughter the air of an extra-linguistic recognition of inauthenticity.

CONCLUSION

There is a story about a man suffering from depression who goes to see his doctor. After a cursory examination, the physician turns and says, 'There is only one cure for you. You must go and see Grimaldi the clown.' 'Sir,' replied his patient, 'I am Grimaldi the clown' (Dickens, 1968: 13). This story, retold by Charles Dickens in his *Memoirs of Joseph Grimaldi* (1838), seems credible enough because of our cultural familiarity with the concept of the weeping clown, the comedian who uses laughter to conceal their misery. One can come across the same story told, with the same degree of ironic pith, about both Grock and Chaplin, which speaks of a modern mythology at work that wants to believe that all prominent comedians are motivated by profound anguish. How have we arrived at this idea that laughter is the close cousin of pain, and that our comedy is as expressive of upset as it is of joy? These conventional thoughts are at work behind the most disquieting double act of twentieth-century drama, the bleak couple of Vladimir and Estragon, the tragic clowns of Samuel Beckett's *Waiting for Godot*. Nonsense and quips are the only forms of language that allow them to communicate truly the full and fixed banality of their lives. A traditional belief of the Hopi Indians of northeast Arizona sees clowning as fundamental to identity, as they hold that they are all descended from an original clown youth and clown maiden. For them 'Clowning symbolizes the sacredness of humanity in the strict sense – that there is something sacred in being a finite and mortal being separated from god' (Loftin, 1991: 112). By embracing the identity of their first parents, the Hopi acknowledge the distance between their daily lives and their idea of spiritual perfection, finding religious value in the knowledge that they are flawed; a similar idea motivates Dante's definition of his *Commedia* as a comedy. These anecdotes confirm the great suspicion that incidences of comedy and humour always harbour a deeper, serious impulse, whether they be manifestations of psychological darkness, or a spiritual recognition of human imperfection. When we consider the ways in which comedy is used for hostile and aggressive purposes, or as a means of deriding others and labelling their behaviour unacceptable, perhaps these impulses are not so hidden. From Donatus to George Meredith, comedy is employed as a form of castigation, a means of imposing normative values on those who deviate from agreed standards of citizenship within communities whose membership is well defined. Traditional finales like the marriage are indicative of the conservative and conformist roots of much comedy, reinforcing the homogeneity of the community after a period of uncertainty. Instances of comedy that openly deride ethnic, gender, or physical attributes are acts of aggression that indicate a fear of difference and a desire to present oneself as more roundly human than those in the target group. While Hobbes's superiority theory of laughter has been largely discarded, his view that it amounts to 'pusillanimity', or cowardice, represents the first ethics of humour to couple the urge to laugh with a responsibility to think through laughter's moral implications. In this we can see that comedy is a troubled form, attending to social anxieties and imposing a fictional logic on ill-fitting or contested world views. How else might we explain the constant worrying or fetishizing of questions of identity and place, and aspects of existence like the fragility of the body, the obsession with reproduction and scatology, and continual tests of the properties of the outside world?

We must also emphasize the fact that comedy is contradictory and it frequently works in a way that is apparently antithetical to the maintenance of the status quo. Through joking and scenarios, or states of being such as folly or tricksterism, comedy opens up the possibility of an additional dimension of understanding, one in which language or perception are not rational meaning-oriented systems but have unpredictable applications. Take the joke, '"Doctor, doctor, I feel like a bridge." "What's come over you?" "Two trucks and a motorbike."' In this, admittedly lame, example, the punchline explores the possibility of retrospectively reading the set-up against the grain of conventional sense, most obviously in the question 'what's come over you?', which is both a proverbial enquiry about one's health, and, we discover, a literal request to ascertain the volume of traffic that has passed over the patient. While the humorous effect of this joke is negligible, it reveals for us the fact that jokes are often a formally structured means of revealing the susceptibility of language to alternative interpretations, the importance of contextual referents in meaning, and the coexistence of viable interpretations. Medieval concepts of folly understood this and fashioned from it a theological truth, that humanity was perpetually looking at the world with doubled vision and a refined understanding of its own simplicity. From this perspective, traditional endings like marriages are a practical way of restoring reason and closing off nonsense, acting as a barrier between the field of potentially radical interpretive alternatives that comedy opens up, and the rest of the world that needs to make sense if it is to carry on working.

Finally, we return to the difficult question of genre. Comedy's denigration in academic study is a product of its populism, its association with the lower bodily stratum, and its problematic resistance to generic definition. While the generic label continues to represent a meaningful and practicable brand, priming us for certain kinds of action and alerting us to a different type of discourse, the deracinated nature of comic effect and the permeability of generic boundaries means that we can no longer be satisfied by the Aristotelian concepts of form that persist in most understandings of what comedy is. Traditional generic definitions belonged to the theatre and, as its popularity has declined over the course of the twentieth century, different types of comedy have emerged in new contexts and media that often mingle with other modes and tones of narrative. Perhaps then we need to stop trying to define comedy on a generic level, and think of it instead as a series of more or less connected effects, traditions, and modified themes treated with the aim of opening up understanding for the purposes of laughter.

Glossary

Bathos a descent from the elevated to the ludicrous, a sense of deflation.

Burlesque in the British theatrical tradition, a satirical play that parodies contemporary or well-known dramas, beginning in the Restoration period with the Duke of Buckingham's play *The Rehearsal* (1671), lampooning the heroic drama of Dryden. Burlesque comedies were at the height of their popularity in the Victorian period, and some burlesque revues ran into the twentieth century. In American theatrical parlance, a burlesque is a sex-themed comedy and variety revue with its origins in the second half of the nineteenth century, often featuring striptease.

Camp Susan Sontag defines camp as a 'way of seeing the world as an aesthetic phenomenon . . . not in terms of beauty but in terms of the degree of artifice, of stylization' (Sontag, 1982: 106). Camp refers to a certain kitsch or trashy aesthetic, an elevation of elements of pop culture to a status beyond that deserved by its content according to traditional categories of taste.

Carnival the period of feasting immediately prior to Lent, but for Mikhail Bakhtin and others, a conceptual category that describes the potential of popular literary and festive forms to disrupt the dominant order, express dissent, and provide a framework for the celebration of unsanctioned or 'unofficial' modes of being. 'Carnivalesque' refers to texts, events, or practices that epitomize the spirit of carnival, often associated with the gratification of bodily desires, but possessing the potential to be read as an expression of the voice of the plebeian class.

City comedy a popular form of drama in the Jacobean and Caroline theatre and associated with the playwrights Ben Jonson, Thomas Middleton, John Marston, and Philip Massinger. City comedy is based on the principles of Roman New Comedy, but brings its satiric eye to bear on the financial dealings and sexual immoralities of a newly emergent mercantile class, active in the burgeoning city of London in the first half of the seventeenth century.

Commedia dell'arte a form of improvised comedy first recorded in Italy in 1545, and flourishing from the sixteenth to the early eighteenth centuries. *Commedia dell'arte* is notable for its use of masks, each one representing the distended features of a familiar stock character. These stock characters are then found in stock scenarios and respond accordingly, the actors improvising the specific action and dialogue at the moment of performance.

Commedia erudita the 'erudite', or learned, counterpart to *commedia dell'arte*, and written for the humanist courts of Italian Renaissance princes. Most plays were closely based on the Roman New Comedy of Plautus and Terence and intended for educated audiences.

Deconstruction a school of thought associated with the French philosopher Jacques Derrida. Deconstruction's principal interest lies in unravelling the 'metaphysics of presence' that are said to authorize key philosophical ideas and dominant discourses. Deconstructive analysis engages in a detailed reading of the ways in which concepts are structured through language, an unstable and volatile medium, examining the extent to which the transcendental claims of such ideas are undermined by their existence within the medium.

Drag generally a form of female impersonation, although drag can work from female to male, in which the fact that a man has dressed as a women is a significant element of the entertainment and largely responsible for its humour. Drag differs from the transvestism of the Shakespearean stage in this respect, as the drag act is not involved in a narrative that requires cross-dressing, and, even though no direct reference is made to the actual gender of the performer, the audience derives amusement from their knowledge that the woman is, in fact, a man.

Farce a form of comedy that relies principally on physical humour, horseplay, and awkward social situations to generate laughter. The origins of farce can be traced back as far as the ancient Roman *fabula*, the generic name for a variety of comic entertainments, and the form was particularly popular in France in the Middle Ages. In the nineteenth century, one-act farces often accompanied the performance of five-act tragedies. In modern usage, the term is generally applied to comedies that feature a series of contorted and overlapping intrigues, such as a series of adulterous couples in close quarters and in imminent danger of being found out.

Historicism a critical practice that claims that one only understands the nature of a literary or other creative work fully when it is returned to the original context of its production. Historicist readings of comedy, therefore, seek to relate comic forms to the social, cultural, and political movements of their day in an effort to show the investment and interrelatedness of one beside the other.

Humours the humours – blood, phlegm, black bile, and choler – were four fluids believed to be essential to human health, the preponderance of one fluid over the others possessing the ability to effect personality. The humoral system was developed by Galen in the first century AD, and remained influential in medicine through the Midde Ages and early modern periods. The comedy of the humours, associated largely with the work of Ben Jonson, used the humoral system as a basis for characterization.

Materialism a belief that ideas and societies develop as a result of their material conditions and environments, in opposition to idealism, which holds that ideas or concepts come first and are acted upon to develop material conditions. Materialism is especially interested in class and economic relationships as a determining factor in human interaction. This term is associated with Marxist and other forms of socialist thinking.

Meta-narrative any narrative that claims to be able to explain all aspects of existence within its own terms, Christianity for example.

Modernism a literary and artistic movement of the first half of the twentieth century that experimented with various modes of aesthetic representation, rejecting the figural or realist genres of the nineteenth century.

New Comedy the term applied to the comedy of the Greek dramatist Menander (c.342–c.291 BC), and used to differentiate his work from that of his predecessor Aristophanes (see 'Old Comedy'). New Comedy uses stock characters and situations and is usually set around the affairs and intrigues of a middle-class household. Plots revolve around intrigues of sex and money and conclude with the restoration of harmonious relationships. The Roman dramatists Plautus (c.254–184 BC) and Terence (c.190 or 180–159 BC) used Greek prototypes in the composition of their own New Comedy, and New Comedy forms inspired the English city comedies of the seventeenth century.

New historicism like 'historicism', a critical school that believes in the reconstruction of context as an essential aspect of understanding literary text. The 'new' in 'new historicism' comes from its attempts to problematize the idea of history, pointing out that textual accounts of the historical past are themselves texts and therefore susceptible to the same principles of inclusion and exclusion, elision and omission, as any other form of text and not necessarily imbued with any inherent authority. New historicism came into being largely through the work of American literary critics in the 1980s.

Old Comedy represented solely by the works of Greek playwright Aristophanes (c.448–380 BC), Old Comedy represents the first recognizably comic narrative in Western literature. Characterized by loose plotting, fantastic situations, and scatological and slanderous humour, Old Comedy is thought to be derived in part from forms of ancient worship, especially in honour of the god Dionysus.

Pantomime   used in the seventeenth century to describe a story told in dance, the British pantomime developed as an offshoot of Harlequin plays, themselves a variant of *commedia dell'arte* performances. Pantomime was developed in the nineteenth century, using classic fairy tale plots as a loose framework for a broader range of elements including songs, music hall routines, trick scenery, audience participation, acrobatics, slapstick, costume changes, and romance. A further convention of pantomime is its use of young women in the lead male role (the 'principal boy') and older men playing the parts of mature women, such as Cinderella's ugly sisters (known as 'pantomime dames'). Pantomime was associated with Christmas very early on in its existence, and is still a popular part of the British Christmas season.

Postmodernism   a controversial and much-debated term, now largely understood to refer to creative or critical practices that reject totalizing meta-narratives and celebrate complexity, self-reflexivity, fragmentation, doubt, ambiguity, relativism, and pastiche. The term received its earliest use in relation to architecture, particularly architectural styles that eschewed the monumentalist and technocratic aesthetics of Modernism, appearing instead to favour process over product and the witty quotation and incorporation of numerous architectural features rather than subordination to one monolithic concept of the new. Postmodernist effects in literature and art generally draw attention to the concepts of form and artifice, rather than hiding them, and reject notions of transparency or intentionality in interpretation. Postmodernism has been viewed as many things, including a reaction against the idea of history as 'progress', an idea it credits in part with the development of ideologies that have led to fascism and Stalinism.

Poststructuralism   a broad umbrella term that encompasses the work of a variety of thinkers and theorists, many of whom rose to prominence as a result of the student unrest of Paris in 1968. Poststructuralism is most readily associated with the work of Roland Barthes, Michel Foucault, Julia Kristeva, Jacques Lacan, Jacques Derrida, and others of that era, and represents a furthering of the debates begun by structuralist thinkers (hence the 'post'), who had posited the idea that communication operates according to systems of signs (known as 'semiology' or 'semiotics'). The poststructuralist generation retained this interest in the centrality of language to psychological and social organization, but dispensed with the systematic approach of structuralism, pursuing its investigations in a number of different areas, including literature, politics, and psychoanalysis.

Satire   a literary form that aims to criticize or censure people and ideas through the use of humour. Satire can take many forms, but is generally understood according to its degree of viciousness.

Slapstick   physical humour associated with the early twentieth-century silent film era and performers such as Charlie Chaplin, Buster Keaton, and Harold Lloyd, but still employed in much contemporary comedy. Slapstick involves falls, blows, mishaps, and accidents and demands considerable skill from its performers.

Travesty   while a 'travesty' can refer to something that has been made ludicrous, it also means to alter the dress or appearance of a person, and can refer to cross-dressing. The travesty of dress is a common theme in comedy.

FURTHER READING

The following is a selection of secondary and introductory volumes that consider many of the issues dealt with in this book.

Carlson, Susan (1991), *Women and Comedy: Rewriting the British Theatrical Tradition*, Ann Arbor: University of Michigan Press. Excellent discussion of the role of the comic representations of women in British theatre, including feminist and political theatre of the late twentieth century.

Charney, Maurice (1978), *Comedy High and Low: An Introduction to the Experience of Comedy*, New York: Oxford University Press. A loosely organized collection of observations about comedy that provides valuable insight into many aspects of comic effect and technique.

Critchley, Simon (2002), *On Humour*, London: Routledge. An essential introduction to the philosophy of humour that considers the place of the body in comedy, and the ideas of Nietzsche, Bakhtin, and Freud.

Double, Oliver (1997), *Stand-Up: On Being a Comedian*, London: Methuen. Combines an autobiographical account of the author's experience as a stand-up comedian with useful historical analysis of the rise and development of stand-up from the Victorian music hall to the present day.

Gray, Frances (1994), *Women and Laughter*, Basingstoke: Macmillan. The leading book on its topic, an invaluable analysis of women in British and American film, television, and stand-up comedy that includes theoretical discussion of the gendered politics of laughter.

Jacobson, Howard (1997), *Seriously Funny: From the Ridiculous to the Sublime*, Harmondsworth: Viking. An historically and geographically far-reaching analysis of comedy and humour's social function.

Leggatt, Alexander (1998), *English Stage Comedy, 1490–1990*, New York and London: Routledge. A very useful and comprehensive study of comic theatre organized around an analysis of recurring themes.

Levin, Harry (1987), *Playboys and Killjoys: An Essay on the Theory and Practice of Comedy*, New York and Oxford: Oxford University Press. An extremely accessible and suggestive text that considers comedy as a perpetual conflict between the forces of pleasurable chaos and despotic order.

Morreall, John (1983), *Taking Laughter Seriously*, Albany: SUNY Press. A detailed analysis of concepts and trends in the philosophical discussion of humour.

Palmer, Jerry (1994), *Taking Humour Seriously*, London: Routledge. A superb text that considers comedy and humour from a cultural and sociological perspective and treats literary examples of humour alongside analyses of joking relationships.

Wagg, Stephen (ed.) (1998), *Because I Tell a Joke or Two: Comedy, Politics and Social Difference*, London and New York: Routledge. A diverse collection of essays and interviews on twentieth-century British film and television comedy.

Bibliography

Addison, Joseph, and Steele, Sir Richard (1979), *The Spectator*, ed. Gregory Smith, 4 vols, London: Dent.

Adorno, Theodor (1996), 'Chaplin Times Two', trans. John MacKay, *Yale Journal of Criticism*, 9.1: 57–61.

Adorno, Theodor, and Horkheimer, Max (2001), *Dialectic of Enlightenment*, trans. John Cumming, New York: Continuum.

Allen, Woody (dir.) (1977), *Annie Hall*, starring Woody Allen, Diane Keaton, MGM Studios.

Andrews, Maggie (1998), 'Butterflies and Caustic Asides: Housewives, Comedy and the Feminist Movement', in *Because I Tell a Joke or Two: Comedy, Politics and Social Difference*, ed. Stephen Wagg, London and New York: Routledge, pp. 50–64.

Anon. (1769), *An Essay on Laughter, Wherein are Displayed its Natural and Moral Causes, With the Arts of Exciting It*, London.

Aristophanes (1973), *Lysistrata, The Acharnians, The Clouds*, trans. Alan H. Somerstein, Harmondsworth: Penguin.

Aristotle (1996) *Poetics*, trans. Malcolm Heath, Harmondsworth: Penguin.

Austen, Jane (1987), *Emma*, ed. Ronald Blythe, Harmondsworth: Penguin.

Babington, Bruce, and Evans, Peter William (1989), *Affairs to Remember: The Hollywood Comedy of the Sexes*, Manchester and New York: Manchester University Press.

Bakhtin, Mikhail (1984), *Rabelais and His World*, trans. Helene Iswolsky, Cambridge, MA: MIT Press.

Baldick, Chris (1996), *Criticism and Literary Theory, 1890–Present*, London and New York: Longman.

—— (1987), *The Social Mission of English Criticism, 1848–1932*, Oxford: Clarendon.

Banks, Morwenna, and Swift, Amanda (1987), *Joke's On Us: Women in Comedy from Music Hall to the Present Day*, London: HarperCollins.

Banta, Martha (2003), *Barbaric Intercourse: Caricature and the Culture of Conduct, 1841–1936*, Chicago and London: University of Chicago Press.

Barber, C. L. (1963), *Shakespeare's Festive Comedy: A Study of Dramatic Form and its Relation to Social Custom*, Cleveland and New York: Meridian.

Barreca, Regina (1991), *They Used to Call Me Snow White, But I Drifted: Women's Strategic Use of Humor*, New York: Viking.

Barton, Anne (1985), 'Falstaff and the Comic Community', in *'Shakespeare's Rough Magic': Renaissance Essays in Honor of C. L. Barber*, ed. Peter Erickson and Coppélia Kahn, Newark: University of Delaware Press, pp. 131–148.

Baudelaire, Charles (1992), 'Of the Essence of Laughter, and Generally of the Comic in the Plastic Arts', in *Selected Writings on Art and Literature*, trans. P. E. Charvet, Harmondsworth: Penguin, pp. 140–161.

Beattie, James (1776), 'On Laughter and Ludicrous Composition', in *Essays*, Edinburgh, pp. 319–486.

Ben-Ghiat, Ruth (2001), 'The Secret Histories of Roberto Benigni's *Life is Beautiful*', *Yale Journal of Criticism*, 14.1: 253–266.

Berger, Peter L. (1997), *Redeeming Laughter: The Comic Dimension of Human Experience*, New York and Berlin: Walter de Gruyter.

Bergson, Henri (1980), 'Laughter: An Essay on the Meaning of the Comic', in *Comedy*, ed. Wylie Sypher, Baltimore and London: Johns Hopkins University Press, pp. 59–190.

Black, Lewis (2003), *Rules of Enragement*, Comedy Central Records.

Borch-Jacobsen, Mikkel (1987), 'The Laughter of Being', *Modern Language*, 102.4 (Sept.): 737–760.

Boskin, Joseph (1997), *Rebellious Laughter: People's Humor in American Culture*, Syracuse: Syracuse University Press.

Bracewell, Michael (1998), *England is Mine: Pop Life in Albion from Wilde to Goldie*, London: Flamingo.

Bradley, A. C. (1929), 'Coriolanus', in *Miscellany*, London: Macmillan, pp. 73–104.

Bristol, Michael D. (1985), *Carnival and Theater: Plebian Culture and the Structure of Authority in Renaissance England*, New York: Methuen.

Bruzzi, Stella (1997), *Undressing Cinema: Clothing and Identity in the Movies*, London and New York: Routledge.

Burney, Frances (1998), *Evelina, Or the History of A Young Lady's Entrance into the World*, ed. Stewart J. Cooke, New York and London: Norton.

Burns, Edward (1987), *Restoration Comedy: Crises of Desire and Identity*, Basingstoke: Macmillan.

Butler, Judith (1990), *Gender Trouble: Feminism and the Subversion of Identity*, New York and London: Routledge.

Carlson, Susan (1991), *Women and Comedy: Rewriting the British Theatrical Tradition*, Ann Arbor: University of Michigan Press.

Castiglione, Baldesar (1986), *The Book of the Courtier*, trans. George Bull, Harmondsworth: Penguin.

Cavell, Stanley (1979), *The World Viewed: Reflections on the Ontology of Film*, Cambridge, MA and London: Harvard University Press.

Chaplin, Charles (dir.) (1940), *The Great Dictator*, starring Charlie Chaplin, Grace Hayle, Warner Brothers.

Chapman, Graham, Cleese, John, Gilliam, Terry, Idle, Eric, Jones, Terry, and Palin, Michael (1998), *Monty Python's Flying Circus: Just the Words*, 2 vols, London: Methuen.

Charney, Maurice (1978), *Comedy High and Low: An Introduction to the Experience of Comedy*, New York: Oxford University Press.

Cicero (1984), 'On the Orator's Use of Laughter', in *Comedy: Developments in Criticism*, ed. D. J. Palmer, Basingstoke: Macmillan, pp. 28–29.

Cixous, Hélène (1976), 'The Laugh of the Medusa', trans. Keith Cohen and Paula Cohen, *Signs*, 1.4: 875–893.

Clare, Janet (1990), 'Art Made Tongue-Tied by Authority': Elizabethan and Jacobean Dramatic Censorship, Manchester: Manchester University Press.

Clement of Alexandria (1983), The Instructor, in The Ante-Nicene Fathers: Translations of the Writings of the Fathers Down to A.D.325, ed. Alexander Roberts and James Donaldson, et al., 10 vols, Grand Rapids: Eerdmans, vol. 2, pp 207–296.

Congreve, William (1997a), 'Amendments of Mr. Collier's False and Imperfect Citations', in Restoration and Eighteenth-Century Comedy, ed. Scott McMillin, second edn, New York and London: Norton, pp. 513–516.

—— (1997b), The Way of the World, in Restoration and Eighteenth-Century Comedy, ed. Scott McMillin, second edn, New York and London: Norton, pp. 251–319.

—— (1973), The Double Dealer, London: Scolar.

Cook, William (1994), Ha Bloody Ha: Comedians Talking, London: Fourth Estate.

Cornford, Francis Macdonald (1914), The Origins of Attic Comedy, London: Edward Arnold.

Coward, Noël (1999), Three Plays: Blithe Spirit, Hay Fever, Private Lives, New York: Vintage.

Critchley, Simon (2002), On Humour, London: Routledge.

—— (1997), Very Little . . . Almost Nothing: Death, Philosophy, Literature, London: Routledge.

Dale, Alan (2000), Comedy is A Man in Trouble: Slapstick in American Movies, Minneapolis and London: University of Minnesota Press.

Daniell, David (1997), 'Shakespeare and the Traditions of Comedy', in The Cambridge Companion to Shakespeare Studies, ed. Stanley Wells, Cambridge: Cambridge University Press, pp. 101–121.

Dante (1984), 'Epistle to Can Grande', in Comedy: Developments in Criticism, ed. D. J. Palmer, Basingstoke: Macmillan, p.31.

De Man, Paul (1983), Blindness and Insight: Essays in the Rhetoric of Contemporary Criticism, second edn, London: Routledge.

Dickens, Charles (1968), Memoirs of Joseph Grimaldi, ed. Richard Findlater, London: MacGibbon and Kee.

Dollimore, Jonathan (1984), Radical Tragedy: Religion, Ideology and Power in the Drama of Shakespeare and his Contemporaries, Brighton: Harvester.

Double, Oliver (1997), Stand-Up: On Being a Comedian, London: Methuen.

Douglas, Mary (1975), Implicit Meanings: Essays in Anthropology, London: Routledge and Kegan Paul.

Eco, Umberto (1983), The Name of the Rose, trans. William Weaver, San Diego: Harcourt Brace Jovanovich.

Elias, Norbert (1978), The Civilizing Process: The History of Manners, trans. Edmund Jephcott, New York: Urizen.

Erasmus (1993), The Praise of Folly, trans. Betty Radice, rev. A. T. H. Levi, Harmondsworth: Penguin.

Ezrahi, Sidra DeKoven (2001), 'After Such Knowledge, What Laughter?', Yale Journal of Criticism, 14.1: 287–313.

Ferris, Lesley (1990), *Acting Women: Images of Women in Theatre*, Basingstoke: Macmillan.

Fielding, Henry (1980), *Joseph Andrews* and *Shamela*, ed. Douglas Brooks-Davis, Oxford: Oxford University Press.

Fischer, Lucy (1991), 'Sometimes I Feel Like a Motherless Child: Comedy and Matricide', in *Comedy/Cinema/Theory*, ed. Andrew Horton, Berkeley: University of California Press, pp. 60–78.

Flanzbaum, Hilene (2001), '"But Wasn't it Terrific?": A Defense of Liking *Life is Beautiful*', *Yale Journal of Criticism*, 14.1: 273–286.

Freud, Sigmund (2001), *Jokes and Their Relation to the Unconscious*, Standard Edition of the Complete Works of Sigmund Freud, ed. James Strachey, London: Vintage, vol. 8.

Friend, Tad (2002), 'What's So Funny? A Scientific Attempt to Discover Why We Laugh', *New Yorker*, 11 Nov., 2002, pp. 78–93.

Frye, Northrop (1990), *The Anatomy of Criticism: Four Essays*, Harmondsworth: Penguin.

—— (1953), 'Characterization in Shakespearian Comedy', *Shakespeare Quarterly*, 4.3: 271–277.

Gaf, Fritz (1997), 'Cicero, Plautus and Roman Laughter', in *A Cultural History of Humour From Antiquity to the Present Day*, ed. Jan Bremmer and Herman Roodenburg, Cambridge: Polity, pp. 29–39.

Garber, Majorie (1992), *Vested Interests: Cross-Dressing and Cultural Anxiety*, New York and London: Routledge.

Garner Jr, Stanton B. (1999), *Trevor Griffiths: Politics, Drama, History*, Ann Arbor: University of Michigan Press.

Gates Jr, Henry Louis (1988), *The Signifying Monkey: A Theory of African American Literary Criticism*, New York and Oxford: Oxford University Press.

Gilhus, Ingvild Saelid (1997), *Laughing Gods, Weeping Virgins: Laughter in the History of Religion*, London: Routledge.

Gill, Pat (1994), *Interpreting Ladies: Women, Wit, and Morality in the Restoration Comedy of Manners*, Athens: University of Georgia Press.

Gilman, Sander L. (2000), 'Is Life Beautiful? Can the Shoah be Funny? Some Thoughts on Recent and Older Films', *Critical Inquiry*, 26 (Winter): 279–308.

Gray, Frances (1994), *Women and Laughter*, Basingstoke: Macmillan.

Greenblatt, Stephen (1988), *Shakespearean Negotiations: The Circulation of Social Energy in Renaissance England*, Berkeley: University of California Press.

—— (1985), 'Invisible Bullets: Renaissance Authority and Its Subversion, *Henry IV* and *Henry V*', in *Political Shakespeare: New Essays in Cultural Materialism*, ed. Jonathan Dollimore and Alan Sinfield, Manchester: Manchester University Press, pp. 18–47.

Griffiths, Trevor (1979), *Comedians*, London: Faber and Faber.

Gurevich, Aaron (1997), 'Bakhtin and his Theory of Carnival', in *A Cultural History of Humour From Antiquity to the Present Day*, ed. Jan Bremmer and Herman Roodenburg, Cambridge: Polity, pp. 54–60.

Halliwell, Stephen (1984), 'Aristophanic Satire', in *English Satire and the Satiric Tradition*, ed. Claude Rawson, Oxford: Blackwell, pp. 6–20.

Hanoosh, Michele (1992), *Baudelaire and Caricature: From the Comic to an Art of Modernity*, University Park: Pennsylvania State University Press.

Harris, Jonathan Gil (1998), 'Puck/Robin Goodfellow', in *Fools and Jesters in Literature, Art, and History: A Bio-Bibliographical Sourcebook*, ed. Viki K. Janik, Westport, CT and London: Greenwood, pp. 351–362.

Hegel, G. W. F. (1998), *Hegel's Aesthetics*, trans. T. M. Knox, 2 vols, Oxford: Oxford University Press.

Herrick, Marvin T. (1950), *Comic Theory in the Sixteenth Century*, Urbana: University of Illinois Press.

Hobbes, Thomas (1991), *Leviathan*, ed. Richard Tuck, Cambridge: Cambridge University Press.

—— (1840), *Human Nature*, in *The English Works of Thomas Hobbes*, ed. W. Molesworth, 11 vols, London: John Bohn, vol. 4, pp. 1–77.

Horace (1959), *The Satires and Epistles of Horace*, trans. Smith Palmer Bovie, Chicago: University of Chicago Press.

Horowitz, Susan (1997), *Queens of Comedy: Lucille Ball, Phyllis Diller, Carol Burnett, Joan Rivers and the New Generation of Funny Women*, Amsterdam: OPA.

Horton, Andrew (1991), 'Introduction', *Comedy/Cinema/Theory*, ed. Andrew Horton, Berkeley: University of California Press.

Hutcheson, Francis (1750), *Reflections Upon Laughter and Remarks Upon the Fable of the Bees*, Glasgow: D. Baxter.

Hynes, William J., and Doty, William G. (eds) (1993), *Mythical Trickster Figures: Contours, Contexts and Criticisms*, Tuscaloosa and London: University of Alabama Press.

Hynes, William J., and Steele, Thomas J. (1993), 'Saint Peter: Apostle Transfigured into Trickster', in *Mythical Trickster Figures: Contours, Contexts and Criticisms*, ed. William J. Hynes and William G. Doty, Tuscaloosa and London: University of Alabama Press, pp. 159–173.

Izzard, Eddie, with David Quantick and Steve Double (1998), *Dressed to Kill*, London: Virgin.

Jacobson, Howard (1997), *Seriously Funny: From the Ridiculous to the Sublime*, Harmondsworth: Viking.

Jagendorf, Zvi (1984), *The Happy End of Comedy: Jonson, Molière, and Shakespeare*, Newark: University of Delaware Press.

Janko, Richard (1984), *Aristotle on Comedy: Towards a Reconstruction of 'Poetics II'*, London: Duckworth.

Jardine, Lisa (1983), *Still Harping on Daughters: Women and Drama in the Age of Shakespeare*, New York: Columbia University Press.

Jayamanne, Laleen (2001), *Towards Cinema and Its Double: Cross-Cultural Mimesis*, Bloomington and Indianapolis: University of Indiana Press.

Jonson, Ben, (1979), *The Alchemist*, in *Ben Jonson's Plays and Masques*, ed. Robert M. Adams, New York and London: Norton.

—— (1920), *Every Man Out of His Humour*, Oxford: Malone Society.

Joubert, Laurent (1980), *Treatise on Laughter*, trans. Gregory David De Rocher, Tuscaloosa: University of Alabama Press.

Jung, C. G. (1959), 'On the Psychology of the Trickster Figure', in *The Archetypes and the Collective Unconscious: The Collected Works of C. G Jung*, ed. Herbert Read, Michael Fordham, and Gerhard Adler, 19 vols, New York: Pantheon, vol. 9, pt. 1, pp. 255–272.

Juvenal (1958), *The Satires of Juvenal*, trans. Rolfe Humphries, Bloomington and London: Indiana University Press.

Kelly, Ann Cline (2002), *Jonathan Swift and Popular Culture: Myth, Media and the Man*, New York: Palgrave.

Konstan, David (1995), *Greek Comedy and Ideology*, Oxford: Oxford University Press.

—— (1983), *Roman Comedy*, Ithaca and London: Cornell University Press.

Kristeva, Julia (1982), *Powers of Horror: An Essay on Abjection*, trans. Leon S. Roudiez, New York: Columbia University Press.

Kubrick, Stanley (dir.) (1964), *Dr Strangelove or: How I Stopped Worrying and Learned to Love the Bomb*, starring Peter Sellars, George C. Scott, Columbia-Tri Star Studios.

Kundera, Milan (1996), *The Book of Laughter and Forgetting*, trans. Aaron Asher, London: Faber and Faber.

Kyffin, Maurice (1588), *Andria: The First Comedie of Terence, in English*, London.

Lahr, John (1984), *Automatic Vaudeville: Essays on Star Turns*, New York: Knopf.

Langer, Susanne (1953), *Feeling and Form*, London: Routledge and Kegan Paul.

Laroque, François (1993), *Shakespeare's Festive World: Elizabethan Seasonal Entertainment and the Professional Stage*, Cambridge: Cambridge University Press.

Le Goff, Jacques (1997), 'Laughter in the Middle Ages', in *A Cultural History of Humour From Antiquity to the Present Day*, ed. Jan Bremmer and Herman Roodenburg, Cambridge: Polity, pp. 40–53.

Leavis, F. R. (1972), *The Great Tradition*, Harmondsworth: Penguin.

Leggatt, Alexander (1999), *Introduction to English Renaissance Comedy*, Manchester: Manchester University Press.

—— (1998), *English Stage Comedy, 1490–1990*, New York and London: Routledge.

—— (1973), *Citizen Comedy in the Age of Shakespeare*, Toronto: University of Toronto Press.

Legman, G. (1975), *Rationale of the Dirty Joke*, 2 vols, New York: Breaking Point.

Levin, Harry (1987), *Playboys and Killjoys: An Essay on the Theory and Practice of Comedy*, New York and Oxford: Oxford University Press.

Lévi-Strauss, Claude (1963), *Structural Anthropology*, trans. Claire Jacobson and Brooke Grundfest Schoepf, New York and London: Basic.

Lewisohn, Mark (1998), *The Radio Times Guide to TV Comedy*, London: BBC.

Limon, John (2000), *Stand-Up Comedy in Theory, or Abjection in America*, Durham and London: Duke University Press.

Lippitt, John (1992), 'Humour', in *A Companion to Aesthetics*, ed. David E. Cooper, Oxford: Blackwell, pp. 199–203.

Loftin, John D. (1991), *Religion and Hopi Life in the Twentieth Century*, Bloomington and Indianapolis: Indiana University Press.

London, John (2000), 'Introduction', in *Theatre Under the Nazis*, ed. John London, Manchester: Manchester University Press, pp. 1–53.

Manning, Bernard (1993), *Bernard Manning Ungagged*, Castle Communications.

Martin, Robert Bernard (1974), *The Triumph of Wit: A Study of Victorian Comic Theory*, Oxford: Clarendon.

Merchant, W. Moelwyn (1972), *Comedy*, London: Methuen.

Meredith, George (1980), 'An Essay on Comedy', in *Comedy*, ed. Wylie Sypher, Baltimore and London: Johns Hopkins University Press, pp. 1–57.

Middleton, Thomas and Dekker, Thomas (1994), *The Roaring Girl*, ed. Paul Mulholland, Manchester: Manchester University Press.

Morreall, John (1987), 'A New Theory of Laughter', in *The Philosophy of Laughter and Humor*, ed. John Morreall, Albany: SUNY Press, pp. 128–138.

—— (1983), *Taking Laughter Seriously*, Albany: SUNY Press.

Mullaney, Steven (1988), *The Place of the Stage: Licence, Play and Power in Renaissance England*, Chicago: University of Chicago Press.

Nancy, Jean-Luc (1992), 'Elliptical Sense', in *Derrida: A Critical Reader*, ed. David Wood, Oxford: Blackwell, pp. 36–51.

—— (1987), 'Wild Laughter in the Throat of Death', *Modern Language Notes*, 102.4 (Sept.): 719–736.

Neal, Steve, and Krutnik, Frank (1990), *Popular Film and Television Comedy*, London: Routledge.

Newman, Karen (1991), *Fashioning Femininity and Renaissance Drama*, Chicago: University of Chicago Press.

Newton, Esther (1979), *Mother Camp: Female Impersonators in America*, Chicago and London: University of Chicago Press.

Olson, Kirby (2001), *Comedy After Postmodernism: Rereading Comedy from Edward Lear to Charles Willeford*, Texas: Texas Tech University Press.

Orgel, Stephen (1997), *Impersonations: The Performance of Gender in Shakespeare's England*, Cambridge: Cambridge University Press.

—— (1994), 'The Comedian as the Character C', in *English Comedy*, ed. Michael Cordner, Peter Holland, and John Kerrigan, Cambridge: Cambridge University Press.

—— (1989), 'Nobody's Perfect: Or Why Did the English Stage Take Boys for Women?', *South Atlantic Quarterly*, 88.1 (Winter): 7–29.

Paglia, Camille (1994), *Vamps and Tramps: New Essays*, New York: Vintage.

Palmer, D. J. (1984), *Comedy: Developments in Criticism*, Basingstoke: Macmillan.

Palmer, Jerry (1994), *Taking Humour Seriously*, London: Routledge.

Paster, Gail Kern (1993), *The Body Embarrassed: Drama and the Disciplines of Shame in Early Modern England*, Ithaca: Cornell University Press.

Plato (1994) *Republic*, trans. Robin Waterfield, Oxford and New York: Oxford University Press.

—— (1951), *The Symposium*, trans. Walter Hamilton, Harmondsworth: Penguin.

Plautus, Titus Maccius (1984), *The Pot of Gold and Other Plays*, trans. E. F. Watling, Harmondsworth: Penguin.

Plessner, Helmuth (1970), *Laughing and Crying*, trans. James Spencer Churchill and Majorie Grene, Evanston, IL: Northwestern University Press.

Porter, Lorraine (1998), 'Tarts, Tampons and Tyrants: Women and Representation in British Comedy', in *Because I Tell a Joke or Two: Comedy, Politics and Social Difference*, ed. Stephen Wagg, London and New York: Routledge, pp. 65–93.

Pullar, Philippa (2001), *Consuming Passions: A History of English Food and Appetite*, Harmondsworth: Penguin.

Purdie, Susan (1993), *Comedy: The Mastery of Discourse*, London: Harvester Wheatsheaf.

Rabelais, François (1955), *Gargantua* and *Pantagruel*, trans. J. M. Cohen, Harmondsworth: Penguin.

Rhodes, Neil (1980), *Elizabethan Grotesque*, London: Routledge and Kegan Paul.

Rowse, A. L. (1976), *The Case Books of Simon Forman: Sex and Society in Shakespeare's Age*, London: Picador.

Ruggiers, Paul G. (1977), *Versions of Medieval Comedy*, Norman: University of Oklahoma Press.

Sayle, Alexei (1988), *Alexei Sayle Live at the Comic Strip*, MCI Spoken Word.

Segal, Erich (2001), *The Death of Comedy*, Cambridge, MA and London: Harvard University Press.

Senelick, Laurence (2000), *The Changing Room: Sex, Drag, and Theatre*, London and New York: Routledge.

Shaftesbury, Anthony Ashley Cooper, Lord (1988), *An Old Spelling Edition of Shaftesbury's* Letter Concerning Human Understanding *and* Sensus Communis: An Essay on the Freedom of Wit and Humour, ed. Richard B. Wolf, New York and London: Garland.

—— (1998), *Julius Caesar*, ed. Arthur Humphreys, Oxford: Oxford University Press.

Shakespeare, William (1989), *The Complete Works*, ed. Stanley Wells and Gary Taylor, Oxford: Oxford University Press.

Shanzer, Danuta (2002), 'Laughter and Humour in the Early Medieval West', in *Humour History and Politics in the Late Middle Ages*, ed. Guy Halsall, Cambridge: Cambridge University Press.

Sidney, Sir Philip (1991), *A Defence of Poetry*, ed. J. A. Van Dorsten, Oxford: Oxford University Press.

Sikov, Ed (1994), *Laughing Hysterically: American Screen Comedy of the 1950s*, New York: Columbia University Press.

Silk, M. S. (2000), *Aristophanes and the Definition of Comedy*, Oxford: Oxford University Press.

Sontag, Susan (1982), 'Notes on Camp', in *A Susan Sontag Reader*, New York: Farrar, Strauss and Giroux, pp. 105–119.

Spencer, Herbert (1860), 'The Physiology of Laughter', *Macmillan's Magazine*, no. 5 (March): 395–402.

Stallybrass, Peter, and Allon White (1986), *The Politics and Poetics of Transgression*, London: Methuen.

Stanhope, W. (Lord Chesterfield) (1929), *Lord Chesterfield's Letters to His Son and Others*, London: Dent.

Stuart, Roxana (1993), 'Duelling en Travestie: Cross-Dressed Swordfighers in Three Jacobean Comedies', *Theatre Studies*, 38: 29–43.

Swift, Jonathan (1993), *A Modest Proposal*, in *The Norton Anthology of English Literature*, ed. M. H. Abrams *et al.*, sixth edn, 2 vols, New York and London: Norton, vol. 1, pp. 2181–2187.

—— (1984), *A Tale of a Tub and Other Works*, ed. Angus Ross and David Wooley, Oxford: Oxford University Press.

—— (1967), 'The Lady's Dressing Room', in *Poetical Works*, ed. Herbert Davis, New York and Toronto: Oxford University Press.

Synott, Anthony (1993), *The Body Social: Symbolism, Self, and Society*, London: Routledge.

Taaffe, Lauren K. (1993), *Aristophanes and Women*, London and New York: Routledge.

Traub, Valerie (1992), *Desire and Anxiety: Circulations of Sexuality in Shakespearean Drama*, London and New York: Routledge.

Trave, Stuart M. (1960), *The Amiable Humorist: A Study in Comic Theory and Criticism in the Eighteenth and Early Nineteenth Centuries*, Chicago and London: University of Chicago Press.

Udall, Nicholas (1984), *Ralph Roister Doister*, in *Four Tudor Comedies*, ed. William Tydeman, Harmondsworth: Penguin.

Vitruvius (1999), *Ten Books on Architecture*, trans. Ingrid D. Rowland, Cambridge: Cambridge University Press.

Wagg, Stephen (1998), '"At Ease Corporal": Social Class and the Situation Comedy in British Television from the 1950s to the 1990s', in *Because I Tell a Joke or Two: Comedy, Politics and Social Difference*, ed. Stephen Wagg, London: Routledge, pp. 1–31.

Welsford, Enid (1935), *The Fool: His Social and Literary History*, London: Faber and Faber.

Wilde, Oscar (1980), *The Importance of Being Earnest*, ed. Russell Jackson, London: Ernest Benn.

Wilder, Billy (dir.) (1959), *Some Like It Hot*, starring Tony Curtis, Jack Lemmon, Marilyn Monroe, MGM Studios.

Williams, Robert I. (1993), *Comic Practice/Comic Response*, London and Toronto: Associated University Press.

Wilson, Christopher P. (1979), *Jokes: Form, Content and Function*, London: Academic Press.

Wilson, Thomas (1567), *The Arte of Rhetorike*, London.

Witke, Charles (1970), *Latin Satire: The Structure of Persuasion*, Leiden: E. J. Brill.

Wycherley, William (1996), *The Country Wife and Other Plays*, ed. Peter Dixon, Oxford: Oxford University Press.

INDEX